To: Jasmine

No Cost No Ring

BRELYN BOWMAN

Temple Hills, MD 20748

Scripture quotations identified NLT are from the Holy Bible, New Living Translation, © 1996, 2004, 2007, 2013 by Tyndale House Foundation. Used by permission of Tyndale House Publishers, Inc., Carol Stream, Illinois 60188. All rights reserved.

Scripture quotations identified KJV are from the New King James Version®. © 1982 by Thomas Nelson. Used by permission. All rights reserved.

Scripture quotations identified NIV are from the Holy Bible, New Version International ®. NIV ®. Copyright © 1973, 1978, 1984, 2011 by Biblica, Inc.® Used by permission. All rights reserved worldwide.

Scripture quotations identified MSG are from The Message. Copyright © 1993, 1994, 1995, 1996, 2000, 2001, 2002. Used by permission of NavPress Publishing Group.

Library of Congress Cataloging-in-Publication Data.
13-Digit: 978-0-9 9
Copyright © 20

All rights re
portions the

Freeman Publishing
2261 Oxon Run Drive
Temple Hills, MD 20748

Library of Congress Cataloging-in-Publication Data;
13 Digit: 978-1944406004
Copyright © 2016

$\mathscr{A}$cknowledgements

To all singles: Stay focused on the promises of God. (In the words of my mother) "It's about the promise not the process"! Discover who you are! Never allow anyone to pressure you into thinking its a race! Believe in the power of your "P".

To my parents: Mommy, thank you for always pushing me to be better. Teaching me self worth & to value who I am. Daddy, my first love! There aren't enough words to describe how appreciative I am for you being my father. You showed me how a man should treat me & love me! With my life I will make you all proud.

To my sister: thank you for your example of purity! Your story may not have went viral on social media but it went viral in my life! The second wind it gave me changed my life! Because of you I am able to now share my story of purity to others! I love you

To my husband, Tim! I thank God for the day you found me! You are by far the best thing that has ever happened to me (next to God). Thank you for pushing me to be all that God has called me to be. You're my King and I'm honored to be your crown. My first and last, I love you!

Brelyn Bowman

ℱoreword
Dr. Mike Freeman

As a woman, if you understand the value and power that you possess, your knowledge will revolutionize society.

This is what I taught my daughters... the same knowledge that Brelyn has penned in a profound playbook that follows.

There's a deep power and value in purity that begins in Christ and translates to modern-day lifestyles and relationships. There's value in the vagina, and the street name for that (it starts with "P") that many are unable to comprehend. For the entire existence of mankind, kingdoms have fallen because of the power of the P. I needed my daughters to know this, so I told them the truth—straight up, "You can be a hoe and give that P away if you want to, or you can recognize your value and live up to that."

I explained that kingdoms have literally been destroyed or saved because of the P... It's an age-old epidemic that has come between nations, communities, families, governments, cities... If women understood the value and power that they possess, their knowledge would indeed transform behaviors and the mindsets of everyone, including men. On the flip side, when you try to activate the power of the P or the V without first implementing the most powerful P of all, as in purity-process and PROMISE—destruction occurs.

As a father, I needed all three of my children to under-stand that, and especially my girls. Their mother and I ex-plained their value to them. We taught them that they didn't need to follow the examples the world would provide. So to the contrary, we created an environment that honored Christ and exalted the power of the P.

The topic of purity has wrongfully become taboo in our soci-ety, and replaced by sex, promiscuity and playing the field. So while I feel so much excitement with this purity movement and I'm proud, and I want to get on a loud speaker and tell the world, that, "My girls did it!"

Honestly, there are two perspectives that I have on this issue. On one hand I want to brag and boast, and on the other hand, I feel like I should bring it down a bit. Purity is not the most prominent and popular topic publicized in current con-versations. Today's generation—and many before them—have been spoon-fed lies about relationships and sex. The truth is, however, that every father was supposed to have my story.

Inside of all of my excitement, there's this governor that makes me cautious of those who have not been able to maintain aspirations of purity. There are various reasons that make purity possible for young men and women—but the most important factor is the parental environment (or Godly guidance) that youth are exposed to. I don't want to put my children on a pedestal like they're better than others, however this is just one area where they happened to win… so in writ-ing this book, Brelyn's goal is to empower all who read it to win as well—without condemnation.

The truth is that I wasn't a virgin when I got married, and neither was my wife. But while we were dating Dee Dee found Jesus, and when she did, she and I didn't have sex for three years, until we were married. There is no condemnation in Christ. So as you read my daughter's words, know that regardless of your past, you can begin anew in him, just as myself and my wife have done. The pattern that we started, prior to our marriage over 30 years ago, has now been a tradition passed on to our children.

The scripture says that if any man be in Christ, he is a new creature. Old things have passed away. We get a brand new start in him. We take on this new foundation without allowing condemnation to get ahold of our destinies. In this book, or by our actions, words, or advice, we're not trying to cast any stones here. Instead, this project has been designed to put a different perspective before you, to give you another choice. The point that Brelyn drives home in this book is that no matter what start you had in life, you can still win in the end, and you can still choose to honor God with your body, starting now.

Every father, who lives in the image of God, has a desire to fulfill the fairytale dream of giving his virgin daughter away to her prince. It may sound a little chauvinistic, but it's true. It was in the heart of God, from the very beginning that the woman (as well as the man) would be pure... God selected a virgin girl to ensure that his own son, Jesus, would have a proper start. So, every father who wants to emulate the position and posture of God on earth, has a desire to raise our daughters in purity. There's something abut the sacredness of purity, and while it's applicable to both males and females, we—as a society—don't hold the same standards to men. To have witnessed both of my daughters get married, and present purity certificates to me at their weddings—to my surprise— has been an amazing fairytale dream come true.

God said that there would be days of heaven on earth, and his whole desire was that his kingdom be done on earth as it is in heaven. So, environment is everything. It was my desire to create an environment where my angels (my children) could reside, and not feel out of place. I wanted to create a habitation of heaven on earth for them, and it was so important, because environment is a subtle force that suggests constantly that we're supposed to be like this. If you put a person in a crack house, it won't be long before you find them with a pipe in their hand. Environment played a major role in what has happened in both Brelyn and Brittney's lives.

Through my teachings, and subsequently, now my daughter's teachings, I pray that the importance of environment is one that sticks heavily with all who come in contact. The type of results that my daughters have had in their lives, and their ability to remain virgins until marriage, had a lot to do with the environment in which they were raised, and the mental environments of their own minds. I taught them to be thinkers—to exalt the promise over the pressure, and ultimately they understood the power of their P. The popular contradicting viewpoint that many people teach is to just, "Follow your heart." I learned early-on that this was not the advice I wanted to instill in my children when they had to make important decisions about their lives. Instead they were to use their heads. Environment, both mental and physical, are important parts of a purity journey and the journey to your promised land.

It is my prayer that all people are afforded the same type of parental advice that my children had. The only reason why some young girls and boys have not been able to fulfill this kind of purity promise and path is simply because they didn't have that type of parenting. This book will help, while presenting a different way of life and relationships, practical plans, prayer and scripture to help you—no matter your age or your past—to exalt the power of your promise.

Chapter 1
The Power of The P

For all the promises of God in him are yea, and in him Amen, unto the glory of God by us.
2 Corinthians 1:20

This book isn't about being perfect. It's not about privilege. I'd love to keep it real with you here, because honestly, this book isn't even about me or being a virgin. It's about you and the power of your P. I know you've heard that before right? That *your P* has power…Well it's true, but the P that I'm referring to isn't limited to what may come to your mind…it's *wayyy* more powerful than what the world wants you to believe… and you can obtain this power through a life of purity.

The world will have you to believe that sexual impurity is cool—that you can have sex with no strings attached—that you can follow the lead of Mary Jane, Olivia Pope or Annalise Keating from *Being Mary Jane, Scandal* or *How to Get Away With Murder* and commit adultery. It'll have you believing that safe sex is okay sex, and there are no consequences of having sex outside of marriage besides, perhaps, an unwanted pregnancy or STD if you don't protect yourself. These are all untrue according to God's word, our ultimate guide for truth. See there are so many consequences of having sex before marriage, including disappointing God…some of the major consequences of sexual impurity include delaying your destiny, instilling negative self thoughts and beliefs in your heart and establishing negative spiritual soul ties that can leave you vulnerable and heartbroken. The power of your P is so strong that the world has actually withheld the truth about its powers from you. This book will make that power clear to you.

The truth is that you have infinite power that God wants you to tap into, and through *No Ring No Ting*, you'll begin to activate the power of your P…or in other words, your process-prayer-patience-purpose-purity and your PROMISE from God. Your power source is infinite because it comes from God…and it's already promised to you.

At age 13, I had faith and believed in the power of my *P (promise)* when I took an oath before God, my family and friends to wait until marriage to have sex. Even at that young age, I sensed that I was in for a *process*, but I knew (through my faith) that it would be worth it. I was taught and later learned that my *patience* would be tested, as yours is tested, but through *prayer* I could overcome the tests of the world and live for God. I had faith, that my life of *purity* would pay off big time, and that God's *promises* would manifest in my life. God honored my commitment to him, quite often, by giving me a loving family and an amazing big sister whose footsteps I could follow, by making me a ministry leader as a teenager, a successful business owner at the age of 18, and on October 10, 2015, a wife to an awesome husband, Gospel Recording Artist Tim Bowman, at the age of 22. My prayers were answered.

When we met, Tim had already committed to a life of purity also, and he too believed in God's promise for him—I

2

married the man of my dreams. Most importantly, God delivered on his promise to me and rewarded me for my commitment to him daily by providing provision for my journey. He kept me in peace-happiness-with a sound and intelligent mind—and a high self worth and value. My journey of purity and belief in God's promise instilled in me the deepest sense of self love and God's love. I fell in love with myself every day and my actions and successes were a direct result of the high value I attached to myself. The Power of the P *(purpose)* also gave me a heart to love and show grace to others—a heart of service. My entire life has worked together in a way that has honored God. In return, God honored His promise to me. My life of purity is witness that God's promises never fail. You will be a witness as well once you activate the power of your P.

Do you not know that your bodies are temples of the Holy Spirit, who is in you, whom you have received from God? You are not your own.
1 Corinthians 6:19 (NIV)

No matter where you are in your walk with God, you can choose to live in purity honoring your body as a temple as described in 1 Corinthians 6:19. The devil wants you to believe that it's too late for you. He wants you to feel condemned because of the mistakes you've made. He tells you that because you've had sex—you're thinking about sex or you love sex—that you're not worthy of living a life of purity. If the enemy is successful, he'll also convince you that this book about God's promise for you is also impossible for you to manifest.

I consider you my sister, so I'm going to tell you something my own older sister Brittney often reminded me of through her actions: that I could do all things through Christ who strengthens me, and that the devil is a LIAR — he comes to kill, steal and destroy your dreams-hopes-visions-and God's PROMISE for you. You have a *promise* assigned to your life, and you have the opportunity to see that promise in real life. Yes, your P still has power. As your sister, I'm going to help you activate it.

The "P" here is synonymous with God's promise that you will manifest through a process of prayer and patience, along with a life filled with purpose and purity. This is a promise that God has said is *yours* if you just tap into it. This promise is often made to be more complicated than it really is. Living a life of purity isn't that complicated at all. It just requires will power, faith and conviction. Before you dive into this powerful guide to help you on your purity journey, there are a few things you'll need to do in preparation. Once you can commit to the prep work, you are ready to take this process one step further. Are you ready?…OK here it goes.

Open your heart.
Remove your prejudgements.
Believe in yourself and believe in God.
Activate your faith, both in God and yourself.
Forgive yourself.

No Ring No Ting isn't a book that you read for entertainment's sake. Yes the title might be entertaining and flirty, but we're here to do some important work. This book will be a journey that you take for your promise's sake. It's going to help you activate the power of your P. So get out your highlighter, pen, your favorite journal or cell phone app, because you'll need to note the versus and tips that I'm going reveal to you that will resonate with you. This will be your ammunition to help you along the way. You probably didn't realize what you were getting into when you opened this book. That's okay, because now you're here and our time together will definitely be worth it. Do you trust God? Do you believe in his promises? OK… then let's start with those.

The promises of God are no surprise. They're all throughout scripture. So let's begin activating the power of your P by leaning on five of my favorite promises that God has given to us all, if we just live for him. I encourage you to use these promises as your constant guide and incorporate them in your prayers as you go through your journey of purity. They will give you hope and comfort that God's got your back and wants you to succeed.

Promise 1: New Spirit, Desires and a New Heart

In Ezekiel, 36:26, God says, "I will give you a new heart and I will put a new spirit in you. I will takeout your stony, stubborn heart and give you a tender, responsive heart." (NLT)

This verse assures you that no matter if you're a virgin in your teens, or a divorcee in your '40s, God will change your desires so that you are more responsive to his word.

Promise 2: Guidance and Wisdom

Psalms 32:8 says, "I will instruct thee and teach thee in the way which thou shalt go: I will guide thee with mine eye" (KJV). How amazing is it to know that God will guide your path of purity; he's watching over you and will teach you during the process! This means, you're not in it alone. Again, God's got your back. Proverbs 3:5-7 elaborates on this with, "Trust in the Lord with all your heart, and lean not on your own understanding; In all your ways, acknowledge Him, and

He shall direct your paths." Here's the thing: we live in the world, but we do no have to live for it. The world will absolutely tempt you and try to convince you that you can manage your life better than God can.

It will tell you that *you know what to do, and it's okay if you go here or there.* We are not to lean on our own understanding, instead allow God to direct our paths and make them straight. This means that in your daily walk with God— even if you're on a crooked path, right now— seek his guidance on where you should go and with whom. The world and your enemy are tricky. Once you make the decision to live in purity they'll try to make you stumble. The truth revealed in these pages will allow you to conquer the tests that the world throw your way.

Our journeys are so important to God, that he actually cautions us on walking alone and leaning on our own power and strength. God is the ultimate power source. He also tells us to simply listen and be receptive to His voice and he will tell us where to go. Isaiah 30:21 (NLT), says, *Your own ears will hear him. Right behind you a voice will say, "This is the way you should go," whether to the right or to the left.*

Promise 3: Help and Victory Over Temptation

God has not only promised to provide you with help, but more importantly, victory over temptation. The Bible has already dispelled the myth that the devil would like you to believe—that it's impossible *for you* to be abstinent from sex until marriage. This is simply a lie, 1 Corinthians 10:13 (NKJV) says, "No temptation has overtaken you except such as is common to man; but God is faithful, who will not allow you to be tempted beyond what you are able, but with the temptation will also make the way of escape, that you may be able to bear it." Did you pickup on that promise? That God is faithful and will not allow you to be tempted more than you can bear… that in every temptation—even sexual temptations—he'll give you an escape route? In the chapter on Temptation, I will provide you with additional strategies. Don't ignore the escape route that God will provide you while you're feeling tempted.

Promise 4: Peace if you trust Him

Are you worried how your decision to be abstinent will affect your life? Does the thought of being abstinent from sex make you fear that *he won't love you if you don't have sex with him?* God has already answered those concerns in his promise to keep you in *perfect* peace…if you keep your thoughts on him. Isaiah 26:3 (NLT) says, "You will keep in perfect peace all who trust in you, all whose thoughts are fixed on you!" Fix your thoughts on God, trust in him with everything (even your relationship apprehensions), and he will alleviate your worries and give you a peace of mind.

This means that your purity should not cause you worry, especially about the ability to stay in relationships. God will give you peace, and not only that, provision, just like he did for me and so many others who have joined the Purity Campaign. He'll make a way for you to live *his* way. It won't always be easy, and not everyone can come with you on this journey. It's important for you to know that. When you decide to live for God, your friends, some family members or even your boyfriend may not understand or accept your choice, but this will be okay in the end. See, God never removes things or people without providing better replacements.

So understand that not everyone will encourage your journey of purity—some people will try to deter you and distract you, but as you grow stronger in your faith, you'll real ize that anyone who pulls you away from the word of God is not meant to be with you in that particular reason. God will give you peace if you simply trust him.

Promise 5: The Devil will Flee if You Resist Him

Most temptations are tricks and tools of the enemy. Temptation is how he will attack your decision to live for God. This means you need to fight him with the most powerful tools possible — prayer and scripture. The Bible tells us to repent and draw closer to God. Sin is what separates us from God, and the devil wants us to remain in sin so that we grow further away from God's promise. James 4:7-10 directs us to submit to God and resist the devil and he will flee from you. It goes on to say that we are sinners and we should clean our hands, purify our hearts, mourn and weep... to humble ourselves in the sight of the Lord and he will lift us up.

Fleeing from the devil is not about just resisting him, or telling him to go away, it's also about denouncing and repenting from the things that you and the devil have done together.... Okay let me put this another way—If you've had sex before, God knows this. But guess what? Your sins cannot outdo God's grace for you. When Tim and I first started the Purity Campaign, we received tons of national media attention, and several girls and women started following me on social media. One young lady sent me a message and she told me she loved what I was doing, but she felt that sexual purity was impossible for her to achieve, since she had been having sex for years. I can't stress enough how false this thinking is. God already knew your life before you were born.

The enemy wants you to believe that because of everything you've done, you can't even go to God and ask him to forgive you. This is another bold face lie. Your repentance and dedication to Him is exactly what God wants. So ask him to forgive you. Repent from your past. Then, ask God to give you strength and protection against the enemy throughout your journey. Remember that God's got your back.

Earlier I mentioned that you have infinite power. That's because the power of your P comes from God—the ultimate power supply. To draw the comparison for you, a power supply is an electronic device that supplies electric energy. The function of a power supply is to convert one form of electrical energy to another and, as a result, power supplies are sometimes referred to as electric power converters. Consider God your supplier and convertor. He wants to convert His electric energy—or power—to you during this journey and provide you with enough of His supply to keep you strong. Your role in this is to simply activate the power through a life of prayer, purpose and purity.

I started off by saying that this book isn't about being perfect or privileged. This is because none of us are perfect and we all make mistakes. No matter where you are on your journey, you can begin your journey of purity.

We all have a privilege to do so, as believers, and at any time in our lives, God has given us the choice and a right to submit to his will. Therefore, this book is simply about God's promise for you—activating His power and manifesting His results. The sooner you do so, the sooner you will inherit the destiny He has for you.

At the end of every chapter, I'm challenging you to tap into your own personal power source with your strongest weapon, prayer, followed by a purity promise to yourself… Cool? Your first Power Supply is on the following page.

My First Power Source - God's Promises for my Journey
God promised to give me new desires, help, perfect peace, the
ability to conquer temptation and an escape from
temptation, if I stay close to him.

Purity Prayer
Dear Lord,
Thank you for guiding me on this journey of purity. I repent
from my past thoughts and actions that were displeasing to
you. Lord, please grant me the strength, peace and help that
I need to remain abstinent and honor my body the way
that you do. In Jesus' name, Amen.

Purity Promise
Today, I promise myself to view my body as my temple, and
take the best care of myself.

*And God will generously provide all you need. Then you will
always have everything you need and plenty left over to share
with others.*
2 Corinthians 9:8

Chapter ②

Fresh, Fly, and on Fire for God

Therefore do not throw away your confidence, which has a great reward. For you have need of endurance, so that when you have done the will of God you may receive what is promised.
Hebrews 10:35-36

Do you remember the first time you heard "Girl on Fire" by Alicia Keys? Did you feel empowered, beautiful, radiant, unstoppable, the way I did? "She's got her head in the clouds, and she's not backing down," she sings…Can you imagine that?…Your head in the clouds (with God), able to walk through fire with no trace of being burned? It's an amazing and refreshing feeling. This immovable, unstoppable attitude wakes you up in the morning with joy and a smile on your face, purpose for the day, and permission to be the amazing woman of God you are. This on fire feeling is achieved daily when the burdens of your heart are lifted—when your responsibilities are taken care of—when your day becomes less about burdens, but more about boldness.

You feel *on fire* when you live with values, virtue and purpose and you know in your heart that you are walking with God's promise for your life…and even when you have to walk through fire, you know for sure that you'll never look like the flames you've been through. For me, this on fire, fresh and fly feeling was instilled in me as a kid. I was always an adult at heart. I wasn't the kid who played with Barbie Dolls. I was always the one in grown folks' conversations, drinking tea or coffee…I learned to be a leader early on and my parents, Drs. Michael and Dee Dee Freeman, pastors of Spirit of Faith Christian Center, made me understand that I was destined for greatness—in every area of my life.

This wasn't only by their own doing though, this was of course the promise God had already placed upon me (… *I have come that they might have life, and that they might have it more abundantly.* - John 10:10). The values that my parents raised me by included knowing who I was in God and being confident with that person; the importance of family, honesty, kindness, leadership and integrity. They taught me character—that my gifts and talents could take me places that my character wouldn't keep me. So it's important to have character, they said, because, without it, I could be in a place and not be able to handle it properly.

These lessons have come full circle in my life lately, since I've been probed so much about purity, virginity and marriage. Although most of the feedback has been positive, people have also said some of the meanest things to me, and yet, my character and values taught me to wish them well and bless them through kindness anyway. Although I have submitted to God and lived for Christ, that alone has not made the media flock to me or girls and women consider me an inspiration — it's my character and values. If I were mean with a nasty attitude, I would not have received the same type of positive reactions and favor that I have. Character matters.

People like me and my story of purity because I'm fresh, fly and on fire for God.My parents taught me a lot about relationships—that my relationship with God is priority and takes hierarchy over my relationship with any person on earth. My dad specifically would always say, " Hang with people who have your answers and get away from people who have your problems." In that same vein, "Whoever I listen to, I would soon become like."

I was principal driven and I understood the morals and principals that governed my lifestyle and the promises and prosperity attached to them. In short, I didn't just believe, but I *knew, without a doubt* God's promise for me — if I just lived for him. I wanted to be fresh—yes; I wanted to be fly— no doubt; but most importantly, I *had to be* on fire for God. There was simply no other option.

Winners Not Quitters

And I am certain that God, who began the good work within you, will continue his work until it is finally finished on the day when Christ Jesus returns.
Philippians 1:6

My parents raised winners not quitters. I have two siblings — and I'm the youngest. However, I didn't get any special treatment when it came to starting and finishing. If I started, I had to finish. There were no short cuts in that. When we wanted to participate in sports as kids, we had to finish the whole season, even if we wanted to quit. Quitting wasn't an option.

This became very annoying and challenging at times. When I was 14 in the 9th grade, I joined the swimming team, and at one point, I grew disinterested. I didn't feel like being on the team anymore. I wanted to stop—but it was not an option. Later on in life, this mentality taught me that when I gave my word, I had to stay committed to it; that I couldn't let my team down and I couldn't quit no matter what. This principal helps me with my faith as well, and it can help you too. Are you bold enough to adopt the mentality that *quitting is not an option?*

Oftentimes, on our faith walk, we want to quit when things don't go as planned. We want to give up because it gets hard. But when you begin to look at the ultimate goal—just like in sports—you will become motivated by that promise. We talked a lot about the promises of God earlier, but now I want you to close your eyes and think about your best-wildest-most pleasant dreams and vision for your life. Do you think those were just ideas you came up with on your own? Absolutely not. God is the creator of motivation and inspiration and of dreams and he inspired you to dream those things. Now, why wouldn't he want you to manifest those dreams if they work in accordance to his will? That vision is your promise. Now it's up to you to reap the fruits of the spirit.

I need to make sure that you understand the importance of fortitude in your journey of purity. It will get hard and trying and feel pointless at times, but just like it was for me, there is a promise attached to your life that you can unleash by submitting your all to God.

Another lesson I learned from my parents was to do everything in love. Even when I was disciplined, and I wanted to go to my room to be by myself, I always had to go back downstairs with them. My mom would say, "Come back down here, because when you get married, you won't be able to be by yourself when you get mad. Your husband is always going to be right there with you." I'd have to come back down stairs to be around my parents, and we'd have a love fest, although I resented it at the moment.

This particular value has helped me a lot in my marriage, because today, when Tim gets on my nerves, I still re member everything my mom taught me about "loving" him, and displaying that love no matter what. This is also true for our relationships with God. We all sin against him, and yet he still has open arms, ready to give us a love fest—even when it doesn't seem that way at the time. Realize this: God is sovereign and he has the power and will exercise his right to get your attention, to draw you closer to him, and to increase your faith—even if that means he has to put you through tough times, our allow you to endure hardship in order to do so. God promises to never forsake or abandon you, so when it gets rough, return to him and experience his love fest.

Fresh...

Today you start fresh—with a new slate and a new journey of purity. It's only right that you restate or identify new values that will guide your life—just as I have for mine. These values should align with the word of God, your purpose and the promise He has for your (abundant) life. Whether you have or had parents who taught you great morals and values, or not, you have a choice this moment to decide which values you'll live by.

If you feel that the values you grew up on weren't healthy, you can unlearn any bad habits once you identify them. It's not too late for you, and your start in life does not dictate your finish. While purity was instilled in me since a young age, many parents today don't place or teach the value of honoring one's body to their girls. However, the truth of the matter is, that once we devote ourselves to Christ we have a new life—and a fresh start to live by. This is your life, and remember that you have the choice and power.

Today, is a *fresh* new day and you've asked God to lead you down this walk of purity, so today... actually right here, decide what your personal values will be (write them below), and if you need to do so, put them on your mirror so that you can repeat them to yourself at the start of every day.

My Personal Values Include
Fly...

Living for God doesn't have to be hard or cumbersome. It should be fun and full of life —everyday. To live for God, you don't have to walk around looking shabby, in frumpy clothes—covered from head-to-toe. And you definitely shouldn't be having a pity party or thinking that your life is lacking something. Just the opposite is true. Believers and those who specifically live for Christ (by his word) should be the most vibrant with beautiful spirits and a pleasant way about them... because you now have access to EVERYTHING.

You are the show stopper—the head turner. When you walk in a room, don't be surprised if everyone notices you. As a woman of Christ, every female wants to be like you and every guy wants to be with you. You're the light, with the power of the P attached to you.

There's a promise over your life. You're an heir — royalty—a queen. People know this too... This is why being fly will soon become effortless to you, and those who want to dethrone you will become relentless. This power that you have my dear, is a threat to your enemy.

Shine anyway. Don't be afraid to be bold and do things differently. If all of your friends are having sex—you, the leader, can set a different type of standard, and therefore you don't need to conform to the things of this world. You're a queen, with a deeper value attached to your life, worth more than temporary pleasures and social acceptance. One of my favorite queens, through her walk in purpose, offers a great example of this boldness, integrity and ability to go against the grain—Queen Esther.

On Fire for God...

The book of Esther in the Bible tells her story. She was a virgin who won the favor of everyone who saw her and won the heart of King Xerxes, over all of the other virgins selected to go before him (for the purpose of him choosing the next queen). Because of her stunning beauty and aura, she was made queen immediately. But this queen had a major secret that she was successful at concealing for quite some time. As a young kid, Esther was adopted by a cousin—Mordecai— a Jew, who also worked in the royal palace. Mordecai was the person who put Esther in position to be selected as Queen. Some time after she became queen, another royal official, Haman became furious at Mordecai because he refused to honor and bow down to him, so Haman created a plot to not only kill Mordecai, but all of the Jews. Of course this presented a huge dilemma for Queen Esther who was now well respected and honored on her throne.

She had a choice to make: either keep silent, about her being a Jew as well, and allow her cousin Mordecai and all of her people to be slaughtered *or* speak up about this atrocity— and take it to the king (who by the way swooned over her). What do you think Queen Esther did? You guessed it. This woman of integrity, with the power of her P attached to her, marched right up to the king and put a stop to the nonsense. She exercised her royal power—the power of her P *(purpose)*, and she's now regarded as one of the most respected women in the bible.

As a queen in God's royal court, you too have a great amount of promise, purpose and a huge assignment on your life. Integrity is a value that you'll have to exercise all throughout your life — and that you already exercise each day. God will honor you for your integrity and for following his purpose for your life.

Another important value of mine, as I mentioned earlier, is being a leader—a trend setter—and thinking like a kingdom heir. Leaders are able to inspire, set trends, listen to all the facts and use those to make great decisions.

Although I had always been a trend setter with an entrepreneurial spirit, of course, I had to truly learn leadership. This lesson came from my experience becoming an entrepreneur.

It's no secret that I love fashion. My dad likes to say that I got this attribute from him, since he was voted "Best Dressed" in high school. In ninth grade, I took a fashion class, and that was probably when my calling to open a boutique grew in me. I never really cared what people thought about my outfit, unless my father said to me, "Umm, you should probably change that." My parents taught me the importance of looking the part and presenting myself well.

I learned that I would be addressed by the way I dressed. As I got older, I grew a love for designer clothes, shoes and bags, but regardless of how much anything cost or the social value attached to what I wore—I knew that material things didn't matter to God. I could be a leader of the pack in fashion—be the first of my friends to buy a new bag, outfit or a pair of Red Bottoms. But once I posted the pictures of me in those new fashions on Instagram, or wore my Red Bottoms outside and scraped the red off the bottom, they instantly loss their value. That doesn't happen when we are leaders in Christ. Instead just the opposite happens. The more we grow in him, the more valuable to his kingdom we become—because we learn more, we grow more and we can help others more. So being *fly and on fire for God's* kingdom always was the first priority—despite whether or not I was considered so cially fly.

I always had an entrepreneurial mind. I think I hung onto the verse that says *God will make you the head and not the tail if you pay attention to his commands* (Deuteronomy 28:13). I wanted to have my own, since a young age, and I knew the way to get that was through Christ—so I always looked for opportunities to be independent. When I was a kid, I begged my mom to take me to the Farmer's Market on Saturdays, where I would buy a bunch of stuff-*whatever*—socks, ties, hair accessories—you name it. Then, on that Sunday, I'd go around the church selling my new goods to the adults in our congregation. Thinking back on it, cracks me up now. I truly always wanted to have my own.

I opened Breezy's Boutique in Waldorf, Maryland when I was 18-years-old, and it was a dream come true, but it was not easy. At first, I wanted to simply have a store and be my own boss. However, my mom was determined to ensure that I was a leader. I remember the process so vividly. I found all these amazing locations for the potential location of Breezy's Boutique. I printed them all out, and gave them to my mom, directing her to, "Call this place. See how much this will be. Then contact them and see if this would be a good fit for us." But she wasn't having it. She pushed those papers right back in my face and directed me to make the calls, compare and contrast and figure out which locations would work best with what I was working with. My face probably dropped, but nevertheless, I was determined to become the owner of a fashion boutique, so I did all the legwork to see it through. Then, to finance my dream, I had a consignment sale at the age of 17, and made $6,000 selling items from my closet. These were the funds that I used as start-up capital for my business.

In life, it's easy to simply do the work for others who

we're called to teach, but it's important that we allow them the opportunity to grow into leaders on their own. This very clear example from my mom is exactly the way that God treats us. He can easily say do this, don't do this, and shut things down, when he sees we're going down the wrong path—but what good would that do? What would we learn from that? Instead, he gives us the guidelines and free will to make our own choices. God wants us to make the *choice* to honor him with our minds, bodies and spirit, but we still have the choice to do what we please. I'm proof, however, that when we choose to honor God with our all he will then open up doors, provide provision and reward us along our journey. Me becoming an entrepreneur at 18 was all God. It was a direct result of me being fresh, fly and on fire for HIM.

Your second power source, purity pledge and prayer are on the following page. Remember to keep these affirmations and prayers in your daily routine so that you can live with purpose and a fresh, new fire for God daily.

My Second Power Source - Personal Values and Integrity
The values that I've identified and those of leadership, integrity and being on fire for God are directly connected to whether I experience his promise for my life. I will uphold those values and standards to the highest degree.

Purity Prayer
Dear Lord,
You are sovereign and I know you have created a future for me far beyond my wildest dreams and what I could create for myself. Please continue to lead me down your path for my life and fill me with the Holy Spirit so that I can honor my purity pledge to you. In Jesus' name, Amen.

Purity Promise
Today, I promise myself that I will be a Leader, not a follower, the head and not the tail. I will not allow social acceptance or peer pressure to allow me to dishonor my body.

Chapter 3
Tackling Temptations

Blessed is the man who remains steadfast under trial, for when he has stood the test he will receive the crown of life, which God has promised to those who love him.
James 1:12 (ESV)

Alright it's time to get extremely *real*.

You're a human being— a woman—so you experience temptations daily. God created us to yearn for intimacy and He also created us with sexual desires. You want to feel pleasure. You want to feel appreciated, attractive, and loved. I get it. I want you to know your feelings are perfectly normal. And let me also tell you this, they aren't going anywhere. The enemy is not going to make this easy for you. Trust.

Your purity is such a major threat to Satan's mission of doom, destruction, and failure, so he is constantly throwing temptations your way. When you are pure, in mind, body, and spirit, you have a closer to connection to God and a higher intolerance to everything that is not of God—and to temptation. This is why it's so important to keep yourself guarded and out of situations that challenge or threaten your purity. Think about someone who decides to not drink anymore. Isn't stay ing on track easier when they stay out of bars and clubs? Your purity is no different. So we're going to stay away from the pornography, music, and even the sexting, right? (I know. You'll thank me later). But I am not just going to leave you out there to fend for and figure all of this out by yourself.

We're going to talk about how you identify and replace those negative temptations with positive ones, such as a closeness to God, deeper, spiritual connections (fellowship with believers), and activities that will secure your future and not jeopardize it. I am also going to help you to determine what your triggers are and how to avoid and conquer temptation altogether. Roll up your sleeves, take out your note pad, and get ready to shake some things up in your life and, most importantly, learn how to stand strong against one of the most common tactics of the devil.

I get so many questions from women about temptation because it's something anyone who walks this journey will face. You may be wondering about it, too, and some of those answers will be covered throughout this book. But here are some of the more common questions and my responses on the topic to clarify some things for you before we move forward.

Why is there so much temptation?

Temptation exists because Satan exists — period. He knows your worth, value, and your purpose in life. And he wants to snatch it all from you. The Bible says that Satan comes to steal, kill, and destroy. Satan even tempted our Lord and Savior Jesus Christ, so you know he's coming after you and me, too! We understand this, but that doesn't mean we can hide behind the infamous "The devil made me do it," excuse either. Why? The Bible says as a believer, you have the power over temptation. That power resides in you —it's the power of your P — *your* God power, instilled within the inner fabric of your spirit.

While we are on the subject of blaming things on the devil, can you handle some tough talk? It's really time to cut the excuses. All of them. Satan cannot make you say or do anything, including sex. We have to stop giving power where it isn't due. You're stronger than the enemy, so don't allow him to win. Once you recognize his tricks (you'll start to see them coming a mile away), pray, rebuke them, and stand strong in your spirit. When you stand firm in your power, Satan cannot overtake you with lust, vulnerability, neediness—all the weapons he's used against you in the past. Will he put temptation in your face? Yes. Will Satan place his spirit of temptation into others to try to draw you down a road of lust? Absolutely. You can expect the enemy to show up as cunning and sneaky. But, honestly, that will be easy to recognize and resist.

Your Power is really tested when he shows up as a man who is sexy, charming, tall, dark, handsome—everything you've ever dreamed of and whatever he knows will entice your flesh. He will do anything to make you forget about the Holy Spirit, so be prepared to face and deal with it. But you can't fight flesh with flesh. You have to fight it with the spirit, and this is why living, speaking, and praying the word of God is so important.

But each one is tempted when he is drawn away by his own desires and enticed.
James 1:14

Satan does not know your thoughts unless you show him. If you've given into your desires—especially with temptations that he's placed in front of you—he understands that intimate part of you from that moment on. Just as James 1:14

describes, he can tempt you over and over and entice you with your desires. Think about that loser ex-boyfriend, you know, the one who you knew in your heart wasn't good for you. How did he win you? Was it your fleshly desires—your attraction to him, his money, his material things, his looks, his social status or his false promises? If you gave into temptation with this guy, it was more than likely because you were attracted by something that was already enticing to you. And he sensed it. He smelled the lust and infatuation on you—just like a shark in the sea smells blood. It's important to think back and know what made you give in to temptation in the past. If Satan hooked you with that bomb-looking dude once, he'll use that again and again and again. This is why the promise God made to you in Ezekiel 36:26 of new desires is truly a gift. Once your desires change, Satan will have a harder time tempting you.

How can I fight temptation?
For we do not have a High Priest who cannot sympathize with our weaknesses, but was in all points tempted as we are, yet without sin.
-Hebrews 4:15

We can handle temptation just the way Jesus did.
Avoid it.
Lean on God's word.
Denounce it.
Know your triggers.

Jesus is such a G. He was in the wilderness fasting for forty days and nights and was tempted by the devil at the point where he probably desired food more than ever. How would you feel if you were fasting for forty days? Weak in

26

your flesh, perhaps? Jesus probably felt weak, too. But he didn't sin. Not once. Thankfully, we have His Word as a very practical guide to show us how to also overcome the devil's attempts to lead us astray.

Temptation 1: After fasting in the wilderness for forty days and nights, the devil came and said, "If you are the Son of God, tell these stones to become loaves of bread." But Jesus told him, "No! The Scriptures say, 'People do not live by bread alone, but by every word that comes from the mouth of God.'" Notice Satan's timing in tempting Jesus. Regularly, the devil will find us at our most vulnerable state and will dangle the very thing that we're missing and yearning in our faces. Again, take note of your own patterns. Were you susceptible to sin when you were vulnerable or felt like you were lacking something? If so, do what Jesus did and simply put your promise from God over the pressure of the enemy.

Temptation 2: Then the devil took him to the highest point of the Temple in Jerusalem, and said, "If you are the Son of God, jump off! For the Scriptures say, 'He will order his angels to protect you. And they will hold you up with their hands so you won't even hurt your foot on a stone.'" Jesus responded, "The Scriptures also say, 'You must not test the Lord your God.'"

Did you peep what happened? This time, he tried to be clever by quoting God's word to Jesus (using Jesus' tactic from his previous temptation), but Jesus gave Satan more scripture and stood firm, despite this second attempt. Never will your enemy give up after one try. You have to get stronger in your faith and deeper in the word after you've resisted his attempts to trap you once. He's undoubtedly plotting more ways to make you stumble.

Temptation 3: Okay Love, THIS is my favorite example. Next, the devil took Jesus to the peak of a very high mountain, showed him all the kingdoms of the world and their glory, and said, "I will give it all to you, if you will kneel down and worship me." Ha! But Our G, JC said, "Get out of here, Satan. For the Scriptures say, 'You must worship the Lord your God and serve only Him.'" After that, the devil had enough, went away, and angels took care of Jesus. See, Jesus understood his *Purpose* and *Promise* and he used his strongest weapons against the enemy. Scripture, prayer, fasting and His own *Purpose* were the full armor of God (Eph. 6:11) that Jesus used to stand strong against the devil's schemes. In this last temptation, the devil made false promises to Jesus, hoping he could manipulate Christ into sin. I'll let that sink in as you replay the false promises the enemy has sold to you.

God's real promises, those we discussed in Chapter one, will continuously help you. One of those promises from God, written in the Bible, is if you resist the devil he will flee from you. Darkness doesn't understand light. So if you just remain in God's light and care, you will find relief from any temptation you're up against.

Why does temptation come when I'm trying to do the right thing?

A wise preacher once said that when we declare what we aren't going to do, we are most vulnerable to Satan's attacks. In other words, don't underestimate your weakness, because your enemy can become very clever in his attempts to make you stumble. This is true for Peter—the disciple who betrayed and denied Jesus three times before he was crucified. At the last supper, Jesus told his disciples "one of you

28

will deny me three times before the rooster crows." Peter was adamant that he would not be the one to betray Jesus, but then he found himself in a few hard situations, and he did just that—denied that he had been a disciple and follower of Christ.

When you're determined to live for God and live out your purity pledge, Satan will become more clever in his attempts to stump you and make *you* deny Jesus and His promise for you. So you have to do a few things in advance to resist temptation:

Exalt the Promise Over the Pressure

Inside of every temptation there will be pressure. The pressure will tell you things like, *All my friends are doing it. I can handle this situation. This guy is really special and he's going to be my husband anyway, so why not just have sex, now so that I can keep him around? I have to try it out—at least once! Sex is a normal part of life*. However, the *Promise* will remind you that you live in this world but not of it, to walk by the spirit and you will not carry out the desires of the flesh (Gal. 5:16), and that the Lord knows how to rescue the Godly from temptation (2 Peter 2:9).

You must always exalt the Promise. Every day, you're simply one step closer to God's promise for your life and you have to be willing to have patience in your process. You have to know that as you are faithful and loyal to God, He will be the same way to you. Always remember when your Promise no longer trumps the pressure, you are subject to fail.

2. Set Guidelines and Boundaries

This step is all about being real with yourself. If you can't handle *Netflix and Chill*—in the literal sense, then you shouldn't be Netflixing and Chilling. PERIOD. When Tim and I were dating, we held hands, hugged, and kissed, but after a while, even the kissing became a little heavy—so we had to stop. This might be the same or you. Set boundaries for your dating life. Also, look at your circle. It probably isn't a good idea to hang around the girl who sleeps with everyone, because she will not value your choice to honor your body if she isn't on that path as well. You know that when you hang out with certain people, certain things are likely to happen. If those things don't honor your commitment and relationship with God, you shouldn't even go down that road.

In economics, there's the Law of Diminishing Returns, which states that adding more of one factor of production, while holding all others constant, will at some point yield lower incremental per-unit returns. Basically, if something ceases to accomplish what you want it to accomplish, it will decrease in value to you. Therefore, if you're kissing-hugging-rubbing, yet your spirit and flesh want more, you'll eventually give in and do more. So keep your thoughts on God and living the life He created you to have. As you do, your spirit will grow stronger and sin will become less appealing. That's the way to remain committed to the boundaries you set.

3. Know Your Triggers

Along these same lines, you have to know your triggers. What tempts you? What makes you want to take it to the next level? Is it drinking or hanging with the wrong people at certain places? Is it watching certain television shows or listening to certain songs? Know what makes you tick and then you'll know how to avoid those things that entice you to turn away from God. If your trigger is loneliness or the need for intimacy, I can promise you that the Holy Spirit can cover that, too. You just have to be open and willing to accept His word and will in your spirit. If you find yourself feeling down because of a lack of physical companionship, I encourage you to draw closer to God. James 4:8 says, "Come close to God, and God will come close to you"; 2 Chronicles 15:2 assures us that, "the LORD is with you when you are with Him. And if you seek Him, He will let you find Him..."

Consequences of Giving into Temptation

Impurity draws a wedge between you and God. James 5:16 says that the prayers of the righteous availeth much. That means that those whose lives are pure have a closer connection and response rate from God through prayer. Giving into sexual temptation only draws a wedge between you and Him.

Another consequence of giving into sexual temptation is that it truly messes with your mind. Ever notice how you catch feelings for someone right after you become intimate with them? You want to know where he is, who he's with, why he isn't calling you. No, you aren't *crazy* or *obsessed* or *sprung*. You've developed a sexual and spiritual soul tie with that person. Your spirits have transferred to each other — that person has become a part of you—all their baggage, energy, exes, or baby-mama drama is now interwoven in your spirit and it begins to take a toll on your emotions. The more you engage in that act, the more intense it becomes. This tie grows deeper with every interaction and it's a slow process, but eventually this soul tie can become harmful and begin to decay *your true soul.*

If this purity journey is sounding like purging —that's because it is. This is a process to clean house and to get rid of who and what doesn't belong, depending on how you live now. I'm here to help you along this journey, but most importantly God is here.

Before we close the discussion on temptation, I want

to offer a bit of advice. If you're in a relationship, and there's a negative soul tie with someone that you know you shouldn't be with or that you won't marry, leaving that person will be like cutting off an addiction. People are addictive, and once you stop indulging in your boyfriend or boo, you will feel it. It will be painful for you to pull back and withdraw from them, no different from cigarettes, drugs, or alcohol.

I encourage you to dive deeper into the Word to strengthen your spirit. Begin to fast—you may want to try the Daniel's Fast and just eat vegetables and drink water for ten or twenty-one days, or perhaps do a cultural fast to rid your psyche of all images, places, music, and media that is not of God. Pray to speak to God and meditate to hear Him speaking to you. You also need to intentionally replace the bad habits, temptations, and soul ties with positive habits, such as daily prayer time, prayer group, studying a new subject, a class, or gym routine. When you are intentional about replacing negative temptations with positive ones, you will be more successful and less likely to pick up any additional bad habits, such as binge eating. You don't want to find yourself trading in one horrible routine for another, so be mindful of that.

Know this—I have your back. I know that if you refer to this chapter and the verses and examples here, you'll have enough strength to resist temptation. Now let's tap into your next power source.

My Third Power Source - God Has Made Me Stronger than Temptation

No matter what temptations I have faced in the past, today is a new day. I know for sure that God has given me the power over my temptation if I resist, praise, pray, set boundaries, know my triggers, and replace my bad habits with positive ones.

Purity Prayer

Dear Lord,

Thank you for your Word and truth. 2 Peter 2:9 tells me that you will rescue the godly from temptation. I am depending on you to guide me and rescue me as I face all of the tricks that my enemy has prepared for me. Thank you.

In Jesus' name, Amen.

Purity Promise

Today, I promise myself that I will stand strong against temptation and remove myself from any situations that threaten my honor to God and His promise for my life.

My Third Power Source - God Has Made Me Stronger than Temptation

No matter what temptations I have faced in the past, today is a new day. I know for sure that God has given me the power over any temptation if I resist, please, pray, set boundaries, know my triggers, and replace my bad habits with positive ones.

Purity Prayer

Dear Lord,

Thank you for your Word and truth. 2 Peter 2:9 tells me that you will rescue the godly from temptation. I am depending on you to guide me and rescue me as I face all of the tricks that my enemy has prepared for me. Thank you.

In Jesus' name, Amen.

Purity Promise

Today, I promise myself that I will stand strong against temptation and remove myself from any situations that threaten my honor to God and His promise for my life.

From Brittney, with love...

Hello Beautiful!

I'm Brittney Borders, Brelyn's older sister. I had to talk with you for a moment, just to give you another perspective about this journey. The path to purity can be a very interesting and it's not without challenges. Like most new things you begin, you start out excited, motivated, pumped, and ready to tackle every obstacle. Think about when you decide to get healthy and maybe lose a little weight. You purchase every book and magazine on fitness, you Google meal plans, and you read every blog and scroll through every social media feed you can find with a before and after picture and a salad in it. There's dance instructional DVDs, the stickers and images for a vision board, all the cute, matching workout clothes, and motivational teachings. You're ready and you hit the ground running. Hard. We all start off strong and then, suddenly, you realize all the work involved, and the road ahead starts to look longer and longer. Now you see this about a lot more than some cute, hot pink sneakers and a few Zumba classes. This is hard. The amount of energy required is more than you really wanted to dedicate. You have been stretching for two weeks and STILL don't have your split. You look extremely together in your athletic gear, but can't run a mile to save your life. If you've decided to live pure, maybe you are the only one not coupled on a date because your "bae" could not handle all of your terms and conditions. So now what?

Now, it is time to find your "why."

There are many different reasons that will motivate a person to persevere no matter what the task. Locate and grab a tight hold onto your why. It is imperative to keep the end goal ahead of you and continue to remind yourself why you are doing what you set out to do, regardless of what seems to stand in the way.

Growing up, my why on my path to purity changed a few times. At first, I was terrified of my father. He is a pretty big guy, with a long arm reach, a voice that can pierce your spirit, and a look that will intimidate another grown man. Naturally, a young girl decided to go with her instincts and stay on the inside of the fence. The funny part about it is that my father is or was not that demanding concerning the topic. There was never any phrase along the lines of "Stay a virgin, or else!!" That was just a pressure that I put on myself. I remember being in college and a friend of mine said, "You are always talking about what your daddy said. It's time for you to live a little!" But facing my father wasn't worth it to me. I was too smart not to know there would be serious repercussions for going against his wishes for me to remain a virgin until marriage. The thought of that alone sustained me for a few years.

Not too long after the fear of my father subsided, the fear of what could happen to me kicked in and quickly became my why. I was definitely "that kid." I would ruin everyone's excitement with two small words—"What if?". There were times when I wanted to go to a house party or somewhere my parents would not approve of, and the thought, "What if I get shot while I'm there?" or "What if I get in an accident on a road that I can't explain?" or "What if on my first time having sex, I end up with triplets?" I did not want to explain any of those consequences, so I always did what I knew was right.

Moving forward, I became more acquainted with my dad and everything that he taught me. I began to see that all of his lessons and his love and his leadership, reflected that of our heavenly father. I saw the connection in many ways and was amazed at the thought of my dad being an earthly example of my father. All of the things that I was doing to please my dad were truly designed to please God. I realized that the unconditional love of my dad resembled that of God's love for me. All of the things my dad so willingly gave were not even close to what God had to offer. The magnitude of that revelation sank in and I became floored with who God really was. The thought of being able to give back to Him, something that is seemingly so small, meant the world to me. The awe of God finally became my why and that remains my reason today.

Sometimes the why can become cloudy and it's easier to get off track, but I set guidelines to follow and obstacles to avoid, helping to protect myself from falling into an unsatisfying spiral of temporary pleasure. It's easy to say, "God's love for me is enough to keep me," but in all reality, sometimes God can be put on the back burner. God knowing your heart and who you really desire to become seems like enough for a while. My relationship with God is an active, working one that needs attention daily. When everything is going wrong and temptations are seemingly getting the best of me, I step back, look at the situation, and evaluate what would be the best way to handle it. When I'm "off" in my spirit, most of the time, it's because I have missed quality time in nurturing my relationship with the Big Man. I call it being "out of my zone."

I thank God for my little sister. She was motivation for me because I knew she looked up to me and I wanted to be the best example I could be. There are six years between us and I treated her like my daughter. I wanted to take the best of care of her. She followed and mimicked everything I did and she thought I was the best ever. I am very proud of her bringing attention to the word about this walk of purity and making Jesus famous. I now have twin girls that I pray will walk in the path that has been laid for them. This walk is not just for girls, but it will be taught to my future sons as well.

Many think this journey ends after you say, "I do," but I realize that my singleness prepared me even the more for my marriage. I was pure in singleness and now I am pure in marriage. My life is lived to glorify God in my body.

I know you can do this!

Love,

Brittney

Chapter 4
Path to Purity

"So flee youthful passions and pursue righteousness, faith, love, and peace, along with those who call on the Lord from a pure heart."
2 Timothy 2:22

There's one day that sticks out to me more than many others from my childhood. I had braces and I was thirteen years old. I was extremely excited, and I felt and looked beautiful. I wore a big ivory ball gown draped in crystals. My hair was done really pretty and I was glowing. It was the day I took my purity covenant.

Purity covenants are a tradition in the Christian and Jewish faiths. In a covenant, youth pledge to abstain from sex until marriage. Many couples make purity pledges before one another as a way to promise their purity and commitment to each other and God. The day of my purity covenant was a *really big deal.* Not only were we celebrating my Promise, but it was my birthday, too. We had a big dinner and all of my close friends and family were there to have fun for my double occasion. I remembered the day my older siblings took their purity covenants, and I had been looking forward to this day for months. For both my older brother and sister, I remembered everyone celebrating and honoring them, and I espe cially remembered the outpouring of gifts and their fancy rings. It was my turn to take the oath before God and my family and to be spotlighted for entering womanhood. Over the years, many people have asked me about this day. They tend to ask if I was nervous to take the oath or if I had any apprehensions. At that age, the answer was honestly no. I was more excited than anything. I never thought twice about it. Purity covenants were a tradition in the Freeman household — one of honor, dignity, and a rite of passage per se. That day, I officially became a teenager and committed to remaining a virgin until I met my husband. After I took that vow, I was confident that I would never break it.

My parents prepared me very well. Since purity covenants were a tradition in my household, as the youngest, I knew I would follow in my siblings' footsteps, years before it actually happened. Although sex was obviously something I wouldn't be doing, my parents never treated sex as taboo. We talked about the significance of sex and the consequences of doing it too soon. My parents were open about sex and intimacy and we learned the importance of honoring our bodies the way God wanted us to. I was able to see the results of purity in my siblings' lives as well. My sister, Brittney, was six years older than me, and her life always seemed fun, drama free, and vibrant. She was celebrated for being an amazing young woman—in every aspect of her life—and I always associated that with the way we were raised and her decision to honor God. Brittney made living for God fun and easy and that was exciting for me. Who doesn't want to be like their older sister? Maintaining my purity never looked or felt like a burden, more so, just a part of life. Purity was engrained and instilled in us. It felt like the most natural thing in the world to me and I never questioned my commitment to my family, myself, or to God.

The family atmosphere in our home only enhanced my journey. We were very close and, in some ways, old-fashioned. We didn't have televisions in our bedrooms, and we had one main television area where we would come together as a family. Family really defined everything for us. I also was homeschooled for many years. I worked around the church and I hung with my family a lot. I've come to realize that the results of my life and my path of purity came easily because of the environment in which I was raised.

Every family is different, and I'm blessed to have the type of family experiences that I did — and to see and live the results of that as I now begin to think about starting my own family. While my path to purity was well-planned and presented to me, I know that your journey may not reflect mine. That doesn't, however, exclude you from experiencing similar results of God's promise for your life. There are so many girls and women that I know, many who are members of my church and are close to my family, whose paths didn't start so easy. The truth is that many women are exposed to the ills of society at young ages.

The amazing thing that I love about God, however, is that it's not how you start in life that matters. The person with the best start doesn't always get the trophy. Now, I want you to know that your environment does matter. While we may all have different starts in life, we can each have positive results and strong finishes. But it does truly depend on who and what we surround ourselves with. My dad likes to use a metaphor that may explain what I mean. If you go into a neighborhood that has a lot of trash on the ground and it's clear that people don't respect or care for their neighborhood, it's easier for you to throw trash out of the window if you're riding through. And contrarily, if you were to go into a neighborhood with well-manicured lawns and clean streets, it's less likely that you'll think about littering. The environment of both neighborhoods will shape your thoughts and behavior.

The more love, care, and respect its residents have for their environment, the more respect you will have for it also. This is the same with our bodies and our lifestyles. The environment that you're in and the things you are subject to will contribute deeply to your path of purity, just as my environment contributed to mine in a positive manner. If perhaps you grew up (or are growing up) in a space that doesn't encourage you to honor your body or to honor God, now is when you can change that. No matter your age, or place in your journey, you have enough power within you now to choose differently and create a life that is conducive and reinforcing to your decision to live for God. Many people come from broken homes, or are being raised in unhealthy environments, but they still have amazing results in their lives. Why? They put their minds and spirits to work. Your internal desires will have to line up with your actions, and you'll have to work harder and be more conscious if you are challenging the way you grew up or how you've been living until now. Do you know the real reason why everyone always encourages you to pray and read the word? *Other than the fact that God reveals things to us this way,* it's because these two activities breed a battleground for greatness.

Greatness in your mind, in every aspect. In his letter to Galatians, Paul identified nine fruit of the spirit that occur as a result of living for Christ and within His word. The fruit of the spirit include love, joy, peace, forbearance, kindness, goodness, faithfulness, gentleness, and self-control (Galatians 5:22-23). If you notice, these attributes all begin in your mind. Therefore, you can begin to significantly alter your reality and create your future if you simply stay grounded in God's Word. If the world around you is war-ridden, destruc tive, abusive, or otherwise negative, when you begin to change your attitude and thinking—according to guidelines outlined in the Bible—not only will your mind begin to transform, but you'll have enough of God's power within you to create a plan to change your external environment, whether this change is a short-term plan or a long, executed strategy.

Don't copy the behavior and customs of this world, but let God transform you into a new person by changing the way you think. Then you will learn to know God's will for you, which is good and pleasing and perfect.
Romans 12:2 (NLT)

I believe that Christians need to stop abusing God's grace. We know that we will be forgiven for our sins, and therefore some of us sin, repeatedly, while we depend on grace to save us. That's not love. That's abuse. More leaders in the Church and those spreading God's Word should be committed to teaching their followers that if we love God, we will keep His commandments. As people, we get tired of people abusing us and not keeping their word, but we don't keep our word to God. He is our creator and the giver of life and all of the amazing things in it. If we as humans get hurt and turned off completely when we are mistreated, why do we think that God is okay with this? That isn't the proper way to foster a good relationship with our creator. A great relationship is a two-way street. If you create an environment that allows you to honor yourself and honor God, you will open yourself to so many of God's blessings and favor that you'll experience an overflow.

Below, I want you to identify the parts of your environment that you can change or alter so that it's more conducive to your life of purity. The journey of a thousand miles begins with one step. This is your first step. Your mental, physical, and spiritual environment has to be conducive to the Holy Spirit. God is always speaking to us, however, sometimes the clutter of outside influences affects our ability to hear Him. Examine your mind (thoughts); physical environment (people and places), and spiritual life (prayer and meditation) to determine what you need to do to create an environment that will usher in and support your path to purity.

Creating a Pure Environment

I can improve my mental environment by

_____

_____

_____

_____

_____

I can improve my physical environment by

_____

_____

_____

_____

I can improve my spiritual environment by

_____

_____

_____

_____

My Fourth Power Source - My Environment
Supports Purity

No matter my past, God has given me the power to finish strong. I will create an environment that supports my personal change and growth in God.

Purity Prayer

Dear Lord,

I demand and declare my spiritual, mental, and physical environment will usher in the Holy Spirit and support my path to purity. I declare the strength, blessings, and control over my environment as described in Psalm 1:1-6:

"Blessed is the man who walks not in the counsel of the wicked, nor stands in the way of sinners, nor sits in the seat of scoffers; but his delight is in the law of the Lord, and on his law he meditates day and night. He is like a tree planted by streams of water that yields its fruit in its season, and its leaf does not wither. In all that he does, he prospers. The wicked are not so, but are like chaff that the wind drives away. Therefore the wicked will not stand in the judgment, nor sinners in the congregation of the righteous; ..."

I denounce all wickedness in my current environment and bind all unholy influences in Jesus' name. Amen.

Purity Promise

Today, I promise myself that I will be proactive in controlling my mental, physical, and spiritual environments. I will seek God in all that I do and depend on the Holy Spirit to guide me as I live a life of purity.

Chapter 5
Purpose-driven Dating

Do not be deceived: Bad company ruins good morals.
1 Corinthians 15:33

Girls in elementary school begin to feel the pressures of dating and sex. As young ladies, we're taught that we should date the most handsome or popular guy, or the guy who treats us well and shows us a lot of attention. Girls of all ages feel the pressures of being single, of not being chosen, even when relationships shouldn't be a primary focus. The pressure starts from the time we start playing on the playground and handing out those pull-apart Valentine's cards and continue well into our twenties and beyond. Our desires and what we've been taught and trained to seek lead to unwanted pregnancies, abortions, and sexually transmitted diseases.

According to 2014 statistics published by the National Campaign to Prevent Teen and Unplanned Pregnancy in a fact sheet entitled *Teen Childbearing in the United States, 2014 Birth Data,* black teen girls (ages 15-19) have twice as many babies than Caucasian teen girls (34 percent per 1,000 versus 17.9 percent). In a similar study on trends among single women in their twenties, the same organization compared pregnancy rates in 2008 and reports that 54 percent of un

planned pregnancies by unmarried black women were termi-
nated with abortion.

Additionally, "There were 536,000 pregnancies in
2008 to unmarried non-Hispanic black women age 20-29. Of
these, 73 percent or 394,000 were unplanned." This alone
should be confirmation to all of us that purity needs to be
preached to girls, especially those who look like you and me.
If we teach young ladies at an early age to date and live with
purpose, we can tackle these alarming statistics and drive
home a message of purity at the same time.
Women are taught that the "American Dream" includes finding a husband, having children, a couple of cars, and enough
money to fulfill all of their desires.

We are groomed from a young age to date based on
pressures from our environments, society, friends, family, bio-
logical clocks, and ultimately our own timeline for marriage.
Women are not taught to embrace singleness, as we should
and to see it as a powerful choice. Instead, society makes a
single woman feel cursed or like she has an incurable disease.
This pressure is where we go wrong. Being single is actually
a blessing from God—a time to grow and learn oneself better,
to become closer to Him, and understand His purpose for our
lives. Remember, our Lord and savior Jesus Christ was single.
Being single offers time to reflect, learn, grow, serve, and
truly become independent and even whole, so that when you
do meet the person you're meant to marry, you don't make
the mistakes many people, who date out of desperation and
pressure, face.

There are *soooooo* many reasons why dating with
pressure will not lead you to your desired results! This type of
dating is like playing Russian roulette with your future or taking a dart and trying to make a bullseye with blindfolds on.
The odds of success will be just as hopeless. Because of this

tendency to date based on the pressures we feel, many women (and men) have grown a deep distaste, fear, disinterest, and loss of hope at the thought of dating and having a relationship. When women date with pressure, we settle.

We tend to allow the first person who shows us attention, laughs at our jokes, or demands space and time in our lives to claim us. The pressure forces us to enter dead-end relationships and sometimes marriages. This dating simply passes time, or better yet, wastes it. Dating with pressure leaves women unfulfilled, heartbroken, and constantly thinking, *What's wrong with me?* The true question should be, *God, who do you want me to be?* Although a person may be occupying your space and time with text messages and date nights, a person who does not align with your purpose will not fulfill you.

So what if you're interested in someone? How should you proceed?

First, STOP! Don't move to the "We're official" stage until you have the "I'm a celibate Christian" conversation. Why do we get to *I love you* before we share how much we love God? We are not desperate women. We are fearfully and wonderfully made. We are the handiwork of God, created in His image. There's no reason to rush into anything because we trust God. He is able to bring the man of our dreams!

We must pay attention to the red flags before it's too late! Take off the "googly eyeglasses" and really see the person from the outside in. Find out what you will not be able to deal with (and what he won't be able to deal with) if anything, first. I've noticed the trend of fear being prevalent in Christian women because we know that the ratio of men to women is very few now. But you cannot allow fear to bully you into a bad decision. To honor God in your relationship, you must be open from the jump!

When the time comes to have the inevitable "I'm not having sex with you" conversation, use wisdom. You don't want to seem weird or pressed and get the "I just wanted to be friends," response from someone. Know for sure first that he wants to be with you, because not every guy may want you in that way. Some genuinely want to get to know you first. That definitely comes up in the *getting to know you* stage, but you want to be smart. I recall the conversation I had with Tim about what I was going to do and what I wasn't. He actually respected me more for being so forward about my standards. I was sitting in the car in a parking lot, staring at the Giant grocery store and a Bank of America. We were on the phone talking about goals and he mentioned that he was very interested in me. I responded, "That's great and I think you're an amazing guy, but before we go any further, here's my list." He literally chuckled and allowed me to proceed. Get a list of dos and don'ts for your life before you get to that place with a guy.

It's really hard to build a house in a storm! If you allow your emotions to get involved and then drop the bomb on him, don't blame the guy for not wanting to wait. It's not you he doesn't like; it's your standards. And that's okay, he's just not the one you're looking for. Instead go in with a level-head. Remember he has a choice, but make your standards known before your emotions get involved. This way, you won't get hurt, and he won't think you're just playing hard to get. You must have it in your heart in order to complete the task at hand. I know you can do this. Keep the faith.

Always remember that you are the prize. The Bible tells us that a man who finds a wife finds a treasure (Proverbs 18:22). (Quick note: This scripture has a lot women thinking that they shouldn't make themselves "foundable." Yes, I made up this word.) I'm simply saying if you're always going home then to church then to work, how do you think he's going to find you? Yes, God is able to send him, but I doubt if you want a strange man knocking on your door saying, "I'm your husband." To avoid this, try something different! Go out with your friends, and not just out to eat! They're plenty of things you can do (think about hiking, jogging, riding bikes, ice skating, or bowling). There are many places and ways to make yourself "foundable," versus dating with pressure and settling for any guy that comes your way. Women begin looking and settling for a mate, when in actuality, a man is supposed to find us—a treasure. This explains another reason why dating with pressure is all wrong.

So how does he find you?

A man finds his treasure in a woman with purpose. Purpose is the standard by which you should date. When you know and are walking in your purpose—God's purpose for your life—you'll be in a better position to date this way, too. Dating with purpose is intentional dating. It's not dating because you're bored, lonely, want to have a baby, or want to settle down. It's not dating because a man has *simply* shown interest, says you're sexy, or there's an obvious physical attraction there. Dating with purpose means that you and he complement each other.

There's an obvious benefit, other than being each other's eye candy, conversation companion, or friends with benefits. When you date with purpose, you share similar religious views and value systems. You are what the Bible calls "equally yoked." Women who date with pressure are dating out of desperation, whereas women who date with purpose are dating from a position of strength and promise. Since you aren't desperate (and you are operating with the Power of *your P*), you should only give your time to men who are on their purpose paths as well.

This is why knowing God's purpose for your life, and walking that path, is ultimately a primary factor in having a lasting, loving relationship. Notice Proverbs 18:22 doesn't say he who finds a woman, it says he who finds a *wife*. Which means long before he finds you, you should be "wifey material." Can you cook? Can you clean? Can you pay bills on time? Can you put your needs aside for someone else? Let's be real with ourselves, some of us aren't ready to be married. Get ready and then you'll be ready when that amazing man comes your way, ready to wife you up.

When he comes (and know that he will), be sure that you're equally yoked. It's a lot harder to date or marry someone who is an accountant if you are called to be a missionary. You may have to travel often to various states—and sometimes overseas. You'd sacrifice much of your free time to help others, and you'd become emotionally concerned and involved in your work. Your purpose, almost day in and out, would be to provide service to those in need, based on Jesus' example. On the other hand, as an accountant, your husband would wake up early and go to work, and probably be home by 6 p.m. every day. You'd be out working on a relief mission, while he's sitting at home wondering why there's no dinner on the table.

Your conversations would probably be draining as well. He'd talk numbers and office politics, while you'd be sharing the results of your work, how your heart is heavy or happy after the support you've provided to a family in need. You'd be coordinating food drives and speaking to volunteers who want to support your latest effort, while he'd be gazing into space wondering why you can't simply leave work at work. No fault to him though, because he just doesn't understand *that your life is your work*. And you, you'd probably be bored listening to him discuss the latest financial systems or last-minute tax season rush. Soon, after months or years of this obvious tension and disconnect because you don't speak the same language, you'd grow bored and resentful and soon grow apart. (I'm not knocking accountants either, by the way.) But the truth is, you'd soon realize that he is not the person for you and that you aren't even close to being compatible.

I don't want to make it sound like opposites can't attract or that all couples who are different will have failed relationships. However, if you two don't understand and appreciate each other's purpose, or speak each other's language, the relationship is doomed to fail. (This is why waiting to have sex before marriage is key; you can get to know each other on another level.) Tim and I were forced to talk because of our commitments to Christ which made him my best friend! We love our late-night conversations about life and what happened in our day-to-day. We work in different fields, but we're playing together and that's most important. There's a common belief and question that society asks. I know you've heard it a million times, just as I have.

"Why do good girls like bad boys?"

The obvious answer is that the thrill, excitement, and danger of that "bad boy" lifestyle attracts many "good girls." I also believe that these "good girls" may not necessarily be dating with purpose. If they were, the need and desire to change or groom a man into an ideal mate wouldn't even be an option. Too often, females date with the hope that a man will change or grow to appreciate the things that they do if they just "love them" or show them a different side of life. This type of thinking is all wrong, because it's impossible to change a man or his desires. Instead of dating with these types of pressures at hand, simply start living your purpose and see who you'll meet while you're on that path. You don't have to change a man or influence his beliefs or interests—that's God's job.

Maybe you're in a relationship with someone who you're trying to change and what to get out. I KNOW it's not easy because you have history, you're connected, and you don't want to be without him. I actually was in a relationship once where we had different goals and standards and it started to become really tough on me. My love for him made me want to make him happy, and I started to lose myself. I started to put his wants over mine (we do this naturally as women) but I remember looking at myself in the mirror one day saying, *"Who are you? Why are you allowing this to be in your life? This is not who God created you to be."* This was early one morning; that afternoon I ended the relationship with him. It was a simple, "I've decided that I've gotten off track from where I want to be in life, and I really want to honor God. I know I haven't shown that, but it's what I want. We can honor God together or I can do it alone. The ball is in your court." Needless to say it didn't work out with us! We have to come to a place where our desire to honor God is far greater than being with someone who doesn't feel the same. Know that your love story with Christ is the greatest love story ever told. You are worth the work, not just the wait. It takes work to sustain until the wait is over.

There is no pressure in purpose-filled dating. You have a purpose and the people you date should be on their purpose path as well. My relationship with Tim is purpose-filled and heaven-sent. We found each other while we were *living* our purposes, respectively. When we first started dating, I thought I'd have a hard time with him constantly traveling because of his music, but that wasn't the case. Tim may get booked to go to a church; he sings and I can minister. We work well to gether and we're equally yoked. We understand each other's language and since we both have always been involved in the church, we relate to each other's lives outside of our relationship. We share the same interests, cares, and concerns. God is the center of our marriage.

We appreciate each other's accomplishments and we understand how significant certain milestones are to one another. We can also help each other solve problems. It's amazing how God can connect our stories so that we can impact people. As Romans 8:28 says, "And we know that all things work together for good to them that love God, to them who are the called according to his purpose." This is how you should view your dating life. Your story can be similar to mine if you are intentional about dating and you know and honor your purpose.

Your Purpose-Driven Dating Strategy

When you date with purpose, you realize that there's also a purpose for your relationship. God created the union of marriage, not to fulfill our desires, but to unite two people who can work together to multiply and serve Him. There is a ministry in your future marriage. Whether you're involved in the church or not, your marriage will have a purpose and a ministry that should work to serve God's kingdom.

If God is not the center of each individual's life involved in the relationship, He will never be first in the relationship. It bothers me when women get in a relationship and think the guy will automatically start going to church, being a faithful member, and loving God. Why is it that we believe we can change them after a relationship starts, but not before? God has to be number one in a person's life before you ever consider being with someone. If not, you'll find yourself so far off—so far away from the things of God. Once you get into the relationship, it's vitally important that you remain consistent in your walk. You cannot allow the other person to separate you from God. I always like to think of it this way: If he is not pulling you closer to God, he isn't the one! Simple as that.

We hear that, but so many women try to justify why a man isn't in God. Sweetie, if he's not leading you to heaven, he's leading you to hell! There's no in between! The Bible says choose who you will serve. You cannot serve two masters properly. You can definitely try (and many people do), but the wages of sin are death! You may not notice initially that you're slipping with reading your Word or missing your simple, everyday prayer, but you'll start to recognize a slight change in your frustration level and you'll yearn for sin more.

During my dating life with Tim, we had times when we just shared what we were studying on our own, and then there were times when he taught me the Word. Our conversations were God-centered. You have some people that will discuss anything and can't handle the heat. In order to keep God first, you must agree to that plan. Amos 3:3 says, *Can two walk together unless they agree?* Ask yourself that! How much easier is it working or dealing with someone who agrees with you, rather than working with someone who wants to do their own thing?

When you date with purpose, it's easy to tell when someone doesn't fit into your equation with God. You are simply not compatible or able to commit to everyone. Dating is less about your physical attraction and ability to hold good conversations and more about your purpose and ability to serve God together. So how do you date with purpose and continue to honor your relationship with God in a world of friends with benefits, situationships, and declining chivalry?

In 2 Corinthians, the Apostle Paul states that we should

not be unequally yoked with unbelievers (2 Corinthians 6:14). This is the first standard which should guide your purpose-driven dating. Other qualifications that the Bible mentions are that a man should leave his mother and father and cling to his wife. This implies that your potential mate should be independent and secure enough to eventually marry and lead a household. For our next set of standards for purpose-driven dating, let's look at what Ephesians 5:25-29 (NLT) tells us:

For husbands, this means love your wives, just as Christ loved the church. He gave up his life for her to make her holy and clean, washed by the cleansing of God's word. He did this to present her to himself as a glorious church without a spot or wrinkle or any other blemish. Instead, she will be holy and without fault. In the same way, husbands ought to love their wives as they love their own bodies. For a man who loves his wife actually shows love for himself. No one hates his own body but feeds and cares for it, just as Christ cares for the church.

Your purpose-driven mate should love, honor, protect, and provide for you, just as Christ did for the church and in the way that he cares for himself. Just by those standards, you can eliminate many of the guys who simply think you're hot or sexy. A man demonstrates his ability to provide, protect, love, and honor early on. Ephesians 6:4 says that fathers ought to lead their families in God's Word. So as a potential leader of the household, your purpose-driven mate should also be in the Word and able to lead and guide your future family through that lens.

When you're dating with purpose, don't simply consider the physical and mental attractions, an ability to hold good conversations, their potential success (because what if they never succeed?), or their ability to provide a secure future for you. Instead seek clarity about this person's beliefs, guiding principles, and relationship with God. You need a man with great faith. This is the only type of man who is deserving of you.

The best way to engage in purpose-driven dating—dating that will honor your relationship with God and respect for yourself—is to begin working in your purpose path, and find others who are doing the same thing or who share the same mission and mindset as you. It's true that love can show up anywhere, however, I don't recommend that you get dressed up every Friday and Saturday night and go to the nearest club to meet other singles. That is risqué, too.

In John 16:7, Jesus referred to the father as an "advocate," which means helper, counselor, comforter, and encourager. As you're dating with purpose, don't forget that God is there as your helper and counselor as well. Allow the Holy Spirit to guide you as you explore different relationships. The closer you get to God, the more discernment that He will give you and allow you to see through smoke and mirrors of those you meet. Once you get in your zone (your purpose), you'll find that dating isn't so bad after all—why? Because every man you entertain will begin to share commonalities with you, and, with each one, you'll be closer to an ideal mate. God is really clever and funny at times. He can connect you with a person that fits well with what you're doing so that, together, the two of you can truly honor Him.

While you're praying for a spouse who is worthy enough to be your husband, remember to grow closer to God. Work on you—bettering yourself in Christ, healing from any hurt from past relationships, and increasing your faith in God's ability to fulfill His promise to you. Don't give into societal temptations or pressures to date or have casual sex. Your purity and faithfulness —in mind, body, and spirit—will only enhance your dating life and move you closer to what

God has for you.

There are so many benefits of a righteous lifestyle. If I can do it, so can you. God will give you peace from the pressures around you if you choose to honor him with purpose-driven dating. Before we move on to your fifth power source, I want to remind you of one simple fact: Always remember that you are a queen and an heir to God's holy kingdom.

For this is the will of God, your sanctification: that you abstain from sexual immorality; that each one of you know how to control his own body in holiness and honor, not in the passion of lust like the Gentiles who do not know God... God has not called us for impurity, but in holiness. Therefore whoever disregards this, disregards not man but God, who gives his Holy Spirit to you.
1 Thessalonians 4:3-8

My Fifth Power Source - I Date and Live with Purpose, Not Pressure

I live a life of purpose and because I'm on my purpose path, I will not fold to the dating pressures of society. I understand that if I date with purpose, not pressure, I will be closer to God's promise for my life.

Purity Prayer
Dear Lord,
Thank you for creating me with a unique purpose in your kingdom. I pray that you continue to reveal your purpose for my life and position me so that I can meet others who are working and walking in your purpose for them as well. Proverbs 16:9 says, "The heart of man plans his way, but the Lord establishes his steps." Thank you in advance, in Jesus' name, for establishing my steps as I pursue purpose-driven dating. Amen.

Purity Promise
Today, I promise myself that I will date with purpose, remembering God's promise for my life and not compromising my purity.

Chapter 6
Consistency is Key

Therefore, my beloved brothers, be steadfast, immovable, always abounding in the work of the Lord, knowing that in the Lord your labor is not in vain.
1 Corinthians 15:58

From this moment forward, your past is your past. You no longer have a right to relive or dwell in guilt over any of your wrongdoings, because they've been forgiven. If your past mindset was that of disbelief in yourself, remember that you are a believer, and all things are possible. If those tapes from your past replay memories of failed attempts, quitting on your commitments, broken promises, or sexual promiscuity, today is the day that you awaken to a new reality. If you've had sex before marriage, God will forgive you; 1 John 1:9 says, "If we confess our sins, he is faithful and just and will forgive us our sins and purify us from all unrighteousness." If you confess your sins and turn from those ways, God will forgive.

You cannot live in condemnation. It will literally kill you. The mind is truly powerful, and if you allow your mind to make you feel guilty, and even condemned about your past actions, you'll stay in that mind space. Instead, allow the truth—God's truth and promise for you—to inspire you to yearn after the life He wants for you. Today, now that you are aware of how much God values your consistency, allow your love for God and His love for you to convict you. You are victorious, more than a conqueror.

Romans 8:37 affirms this for you, "Despite all these things, overwhelming victory is ours through Christ, who loved us." This means (if you accept and believe this fact) you are already victorious in your purity journey. While it can be quite natural to have questions, or even doubts, about whether you can live up to this promise, the promises of God should reassure you that all things are possible through Him, *even this.* I pray that some of the previous chapters about temptation, God's promise for you, and purpose-driven dating can ease your doubts as you review and reflect on how much control you truly have.

We've established that you have the power within you to conquer temptation, that God has made a promise to you that no temptation will overcome you, and there will always be an exit strategy from temptation. Always. Most importantly, we've come to understand and know God as our helper. This means He doesn't expect you to face this alone. If you are able to humble yourself, push aside fleshly desires, and call on Him for help, there is no doubt that the Lord will be there for you. Draw near to God and He will draw near to you.

Consistency is defined as firmness, persistency, and resistance to movement. When you are consistent, you establish patterns and habits that shape your character. From this point forward, declare that you are immovable. In Chapter 2,, I shared the "Winners not Quitters" mentality that I learned from my parents. Consistency determines the difference between whether you succeed or fail—win or lose. This single factor is crucial for you as you live a life of purity. This month, if you've decided to live in purity, please don't change your mind next month, or when you enter a new relationship. When you stop and start, you put yourself in a position where you can never see the promises of God, simply because of your inconsistent behavior. Imagine how much an inconsistent relationship irritates you.

When someone makes a promise, fails to keep it, calls you once in a while, only reaches out when they need you, would you feel that this person loves you or wants to have a relationship with you? No. I believe that this is also how our inconsistency makes God feel. Consistency is key in your relationship with God.

If you have been consistent, do so without any rules or ultimatums for God. Many people start living for God and expect it to be an *If this, than that* relationship with instant, microwave-like results. Refrain from putting a timeline on God's work.

If you've lived a righteous life for two days or two weeks, even two years, and you don't feel like God is moving fast enough, realize that God doesn't work on our time. He saves us by grace and rewards us for living for Him—this doesn't mean that He'll send your husband to you the day after you decide to be faithful to His commandments for purity. Now He might, but He might not. Still, you should remain faithful. Don't put a timeline on God. If you do your part by remaining unmovable and unwilling to compromise your faith, God will do His part—in due time—and on His time. Galatians 6:9 reminds us to *not grow weary of doing good, for in due season we will reap, if we do not give up.* This is the verse that you need to keep plastered in your mind. As a matter of fact, put a highlighter to that verse. If nothing else sticks with you from this chapter, remember that **consistency pays off—always.**

I remember wanting to get married so bad! It was like I decided I was cool with waiting and being content, but all of a sudden, I was stressed and worked up about being married. My mentor would tell me, "Calm down, it's almost time!" The Holy Spirit checked me, and said, "Have I ever failed you before?" In that moment I looked back over the things I believed Him for, realized they were manifested, and I GOT CONVICTED, quickly. I knew I had allowed myself to get weary in well doing. I corrected my actions and moved forward focusing on the Promise!

If you think about any success story, those of famous athletes, actors, scholars, and leaders—even your own story—you'll recognize a common theme: You all were consistent and did not give up. Hip-Hop Mogul and spiritual leader Russell Simmons says something that I really love in his book *Super Rich,* "The only way to lose is if you quit." You may have heard the saying that if you want to be something, do it every day. If you want to be a writer or call yourself a writer, you will write everyday—the same is true with your Christianity. If you are a Christian, live for Christ consistently, be unmovable, and persistent. Live for Him every day, all day. When you give up and fall off, you knock yourself down a notch.

Your momentum gets shattered every time you start and stop. Think about a kid riding a bicycle up a hill. If she keeps going, although it might be a challenge to get up the hill, she'll eventually make it to the top if she doesn't give up. However, if in the middle of the hill, she stops peddling, she's destined to roll backwards and lose all of the ground she's already covered. Do not go backwards on this journey. Keep pushing up the hill. Your consistency will pay off.

I know all the things you do, that you are neither hot nor cold.

I wish that you were one or the other! But since you are like lukewarm hot water, neither hot nor cold, I will spit you out of my mouth!
Revelations 3:15-16

Purity in Today's Relationships

Imagine how complicated your life will be if you date a guy whose only reason for not having sex is you don't want to have sex. You will feel pressured, and, at any moment when your flesh is weak, he will gladly be willing to relieve your tension. Amos 3:3 (NLT) asks, "Can two people walk together without agreeing on the direction?" The answer is no. A lot of people don't realize how hard it is to be committed to purity if the person they're with isn't committed. It makes it so much harder, but when you are with someone who is also committed to purity, you will have an easier time together. As you begin dating with purpose and you finally settle into a relationship with another **committed** believer, it's going to be extremely important for you both to be equally yoked. From the beginning, it will be easier for you to remain consistent if you make it clear what you will and will not do.

You should have a serious conversation with each other. He may or may not be able to accept that you are not having sex outside of marriage. You'll need to discern this and truly be willing to put the promise of God over the temptation and your personal desires to be in that relationship. Regardless of the outcome, both of you will be better off if you simply state your guidelines up front. In short, keep it real and don't be a tease! A lot of people don't realize how hard it is to be committed if the person they're with isn't on the same page. On the other hand, what if your partner is also devoted to purity. When you are honest with him about your desires, he will likely say, "I feel you. You have to pray."

Can you imagine?

I mean seriously think about how much more empowered and dedicated you would feel, knowing the person you love is willing to support you, stand beside you, and encourage you? That response will make you feel reassured, supported, and comfortable in your journey—not pressured.

One of my goals for this book and the purity movement is to encourage women to be forward and upfront about their standards and what they will and will not do in relationships. If this goal can be achieved, a lot of stuff that happens in relationships will cease to exist. Women truly do hold much of the power with sex. I've had a lot of conversations about this with my husband, Tim, and he's told me that he loved that a lot about me. From the jump, I made it clear, "Here's what I'm doing, and this is what I'm not doing."

When you aren't upfront about your guidelines as a woman, you will end up with someone who doesn't hold your similar beliefs about purity, and you'll simply just drag the guy along on your journey. Imagine being three years into a relationship with someone who still hasn't gone to church or established a relationship with God on his own. How do you think your spirituality and relationship with God will suffer from this? I've been there, done that, and it isn't a fun experience. It's called dating with pressure (not purpose) and it's one of the most uncomfortable feelings in the world.

I remember breaking that relationship off, knowing in my spirit that I was making the right decision, but my flesh wasn't happy. I cried like he died for weeks, but ultimately I put the promise over the pressure and I realized my consistency to God was not to be compromised because of fleshly desires. Psalm 34:8 says, "Taste and see that the LORD is good; blessed is the one who takes refuge in him." When you rely on God and taste His goodness, you will become ad dicted to how a promise-driven life feels and the ways that God fulfills you.

Take refuge in Him, stay consistent, even in your relationships, and you will see that the blessings that He provides are much better than anything a man, relationship, or sex can give you. Remember that if you and your man are not on the same page, you will not be able to change him. You cannot save a man if he doesn't want to be saved. He already has his own soul. Many women get into relationships and think, *If I do this, he'll do that. He'll change if I keep trying.* No Boo Boo. If he hasn't changed yet, he won't change for you or because of you.

As you strive to stay consistent, your force will be the power of your promise, and the value you place on that. Once you realize the value and the worth of your body and your promise, and make the decision to honor it, you will begin to see results and you can measure its significance in your life. Your value for yourself, your body, and your life's promise has to become so significant to you so that nothing or no one else even compares.

Too often, we place value on the wrong things in life. Stuff doesn't fulfill us—no matter what the *stuff* is, it doesn't compare to the fulfillment that God gives. Stuff may have worldly value, but it lacks spiritual value, and therefore it holds no real value at all. Earlier I talked a lot about purpose-driven dating, being equally yoked, and being involved with people who share your purpose path. Once you allow the spirit of God to consume you and you hold that relationship to the utmost value, those people who only value worldly things will stick out like a sore thumb to you. You'll be able to tell that they are moved and motivated by the flesh and worldly desires. You'll be able to see if they speak your same spiritual language and if getting close to them can potentially jeopard ize your personal consistency and purity.

Some people have grown so accustomed to worldly values like money, cars, and clothes, and have learned to fake their happiness so much, that they've lost sight of what's truly valuable and meaningful in life. While I'm not saying that anyone is perfect, our spirits are reflected through how we live and what we speak. It's all about our hearts and that's what God truly looks at. Matthew 5:8 says, "Blessed are the pure at heart, for they shall see God."

The heart is the birthplace of righteousness, and from there our spiritual consistency is born and fed. The way we live, what we say, how we behave, are all fruit of the spirit. Consistency is key and the dots of our lives will connect once we become consistent. While I know that no one is perfect, I am a firm believer that if we strive for perfection, we will have better results and consistency than if we didn't.

As you are seeking to be consistent, I strongly urge you to allow the Holy Spirit to consume you. Delight in the Lord. This is extremely important as you're seeking purpose-driven dating in the world of social media validation, selfies, and new-age narcissism inspired by the hype of Instagram and other sites where users are encouraged to glorify their material possessions. If your spirit isn't strong enough, you'll be tempted to fall into this dangerous trap of allowing your flesh (versus your spirit) to lead your dating choices. Your consistency will rely on the value you put on yourself and God's promise. All that glitters is not gold. Be very careful to guard your heart and allow God to consume your spirit as you remain consistently pure.

My Sixth Power Source - I Value Myself and My Promise
I will place the highest value on myself and my faith in God's promise for my life. This outweighs everything. As I put myself first, my personal value will play out in the form of consistency in my purity journey.

Purity Prayer
Dear Lord,
You are excellent in all your ways. I praise you in advance for being my helper as I consistently pursue your promise for my life. Psalm 119 says blessed are those who keep your testimonies and who seek You with their whole heart. I seek You with my heart and I ask for Your Holy Spirit to consume and fill me up as I seek to remain consistently pure. In Jesus' name I pray, Amen.

Purity Promise
Today, I promise myself that I will empower myself toward consistency by consistently reading, living, and speaking God's Word.

My Sixth Power Source – I Value Myself and My Promise
I will place the highest value on myself and my faith in God's promise for my life. This outweighs everything. As I put myself first, my personal value will play out in the form of consistency in my purity journey.

Purity Prayer
Dear Lord,
You are excellent in all your ways. I praise you in advance for being my helper as I consistently pursue your promise for my life. Psalm 119 says blessed are those who keep your testimonies and who seek You with their whole heart. I seek You with my heart and I ask for Your Holy Spirit to consume and fill me up... I seek to remain consistently pure. In Jesus name I pray. Amen

Purity Promise
Today, I promise myself that I will empower myself toward consistency by consistently reading, living, and speaking God's Word.

Chapter 7

My Favorite Position

No eye has seen, no ear has heard, and no mind has imagined what God has prepared for those who love him.
1 Corinthians 2:9

My favorite position isn't an easy one for skeptics to infiltrate. It takes killing off things, people, our personal desires, and old ways. It takes a lot of flexibility and willingness to submit and be used, transformed, and loved to the point that we're sometimes uncomfortable. This position will have you wrapped in tough love—sweet, patient, and protective love—and it sometimes goes against our natural desires. My favorite position is my posture toward honoring God.

As Christians, we honor God because we love Him. Our love for God causes us to put God first. We want to be consumed by Him. To love and honor God means that you have to live a certain way and, most importantly, keep His commandments. While we all fall short of His instructions, we have a choice to make and a stance to take. Will we choose God and put Him in the number one position in our lives or will we put the world in that top position instead?

Honoring God daily isn't the easiest of things to do.

It's a daily process of "killing yourself." I know that's a harsh way to say what the Apostle Paul called us to do—to "die to flesh daily," but let's go the extreme route! We must make honoring God a major priority in our lives. If He does not become the priority, it will be easier for us not to honor Him. One sure way I know that you can honor God daily is by allowing the Holy Spirit, our Helper, to lead and guide you in all your ways. I know we've discussed this a lot thus far, but it's worth the reinforcement from another perspective.

In the previous chapter, we talked about prioritizing your personal value and promise from God above all other things. Since God placed a great value and promise on your life, and even made you His top priority as a member of His body, it only makes sense that in return, you make Him your number one priority as well. When your ultimate goal is to honor God, you won't be so quick to make certain decisions.

You'll step back and question what you need to do—whether it's speaking more gently, becoming slow to anger, extending grace and forgiveness to those who've hurt you, or abstaining from sex. Your favorite position, a position of honoring God and putting Him first, will play out in every area of your life. Your commitment and devotion toward God needs to be one so strong that you are after His own heart. This is the difference between God being Lord over your life and Savior in your life. See, when He is Lord, He rules all. He is you and you are Him. You dwell in the secret place with Him. When He is *only* Savior, he's someone you acknowledge when you need to, or better yet, someone you only talk to when you need something.

Just like a tow truck driver can become your savior from harm when you get a flat tire on a lonely road in the middle of the night, God becomes equivalent to that tow, or a mail courier, grocery store clerk, and car repairman that only receives a call from you when you need to be rescued or helped. I don't know about you, but I don't want to just know *of* God, I want to dwell and abide in who He is! If this sounds dramatic to you, I assure you it's not. There are dozens of scriptures that affirm this: that God lives in those who love Him.

"If anyone acknowledges that Jesus is the Son of God, God lives in him and he in God" (1 John 4:15). It is not impossible or even a huge challenge to live for God, because He is already in you. So I refuse to be a simple guest in His house on Sundays or a visitor that comes to Him in prayer once a week. I want Him in and with me at all times. Just like when you go over someone's house, you're considered a guest if you only come every once in a while. They give you attention and vice versa while you're there, but you never become more than just a guest. You haven't dwelled there on a consistent basis. You just visit every so often for holidays, special celebrations, or maybe when someone is sick or passed away. On the other hand, when you become family or a close friend, you can go in their refrigerator and use their bathroom without asking. You know this person and they know you. They have grown to love you. You have a closer relationship than that of just a guest. This is how I want you to be. This is how you should desire to be—so tight with God that when you pray, He's not like, "Oh hey stranger."

Instead you have an intimate relationship with one another. God will hear your prayers and know His child is speaking to Him and you'll have His full attention. Remember James 5:16, *The effectual fervent prayer of a righteous man availeth much*. What this verse is essentially saying is that the one who consistently and intimately spends time with God will also have a closer relationship and higher priority with Him. Now do you understand why honoring God should be your FAVORITE position, too?

Imagine the trust that you build for someone who calls you every day, comes to see you weekly, shares intimate moments, thoughts, and their life's desire with you. Your trust for that person will grow and vice versa. God wants to be able to trust you with the promise He's assigned to your life, and with the missions He wants you to accomplish. When you put God in your favorite position, you will learn and grow to trust Him with all things, and He'll know that you can be trusted as well.

Let's take this one step further.

Honoring God and His position in life makes everything that we've already discussed easier—temptation, consistency, dating—all of it. When you place God in the number one position as Lord over your life, you won't be easily moved or swayed, and anything that is not of God's will become easier to fight off. This is the way that you truly tap into the power of your P. Once your favorite position is on your knees in a praying posture, honoring God and spending time with Him intimately, anyone who tries to talk with you, tempt you, take up your time will get a similar response from you: *I'm honoring God, so if you're not about that life, you have no place in my life.* A posture of honoring God and putting Him first has tremendous benefits on your character and confidence as a whole.

Remember how I mentioned the tons of negative and hateful comments I received after I made the decision to present a purity certificate to my father at my wedding? Well, it wasn't just from random people. I had so many interviews with news journalists, TV broadcasters, and bloggers. Some people would really dig and dig and wanted to find something legitimately negative about our story. They brought up the hurtful comments and slander and did everything they could to get a reaction out of me. I told every reporter the same thing, "When people say negative things about me, I thank them anyway and tell them to have a nice day." The reason I'm able to take the backlash, comments, and digging and still keep a smile on my face is due to my posture toward honoring God. The commitment and consistency in this position has had positive effects on my life and spirit. He gives me confidence and assurance, and I don't need validation, affirmation, or approval from people. What people say does not hurt because I know the truth—the truth that God gave me—and I know I've honored that.

I stand so firm in the Word of God that when people talk about me, it doesn't change my position. It just motivates me to get closer to God and to seek His protection. Imagine if God was not in my number one position. When our purity story broke national, and the hate-filled Instagram comments and condescending blog posts about me hit the Internet, I would've been broken. The exterior layer would have been exposed, revealing a very dense, interior faith. I may have reacted negatively to those who responded that way to me. I may have embarrassed myself on national TV if I was hurt. Instead just the opposite happened.

The negativity only made our purity platform stronger, inspired more women and girls, caught the attention of more media, and ultimately all glory went to God. When those journalists dug underneath the surface of my life, they uncovered my commitment and years of living a lifestyle that honors God. There was no dirt to be exposed, just honest-to-God faith and my lifelong posture of honoring Him. I'm living proof that God's Word never comes back void and my story proves what David writes in Psalm 110:1, *Sit at the Lord's right hand until he makes your enemies your footstool.*

How amazing is my favorite position? The hate that

was meant to destroy me, only made me stronger and God's Word reach wider. This is not by accident either, and it's not just the case with people who've done everything right. No matter who you are, and what you've done, once you put God in your number one position, and give all glory and honor to Him, He will be excited to transform your situation into a platform for His kingdom. God wants you to trust Him and honor Him so that He can transform your trials, your mess, your betrayals, and even your heartache into your testimony. You cannot lose once God becomes your number one priority.

If you develop a personal belief system that is rooted in God's Word and stand strong in what you believe, then people won't be able to sway you left or right. They won't be able to hurt your feelings very easily and they won't be able to mistreat you. When you make a posture of honoring God and you put His promise for your life above everything else, you will hold onto Him so tightly that people won't be able to mistreat and abuse you any longer. You will now know that you have a promise attached to you and you will become so committed to honoring God and pursuing that promise that you won't become side tracked. Can you envision having that much fortitude, faith, and focus?

Becoming Proactive about How You're Treated

As you should know by now, you're a queen with an inheritance, an heir to God's holy kingdom. Now for one moment, I want you to simply think back to the last time someone didn't treat you so queenly. How long did you stay around a person or people who hurt you and didn't value your worth? What finally made you leave their presence? Was it because you suddenly valued your own worth or you realized that this person would never put you in the position that you knew you deserved? This theme—of becoming brokenhearted, reaching spiritual and mental rock-bottom, finally recognizing our self-worth, eventually becoming fed up and intolerant to the mistreatment—is a common experience shared among many women who've fell into the wrong relationships.

Some women take longer than others to realize their worth in Christ, but once they do, they often become a new person with a renewed mind and spirit. Some women get fed up temporarily but they refuse to allow Christ to consume that number one position. So they continuously go down the same paths, making the same mistakes, and are treated like peasants, rather than queens, without learning the lessons God so desperately wants to teach them.

We have to begin to recognize this in ourselves and our sisters and become each other's support system. I'm writing this book and sharing the spiritual strategies that I've lived by, so that I can support you and do my best to prevent you from experiencing repeated heartbreak because of your flesh. Instead I really want you to experience God's promise by living through the spirit. I want you to realize this one thing: You're a diamond, not a piece of glass. Think about how diamonds are treated. They're something to aspire for, to work for, to save up money to purchase. We shine them, show them off, value them, and ensure that we don't misplace or mistreat them. Glass on the other hand is kicked around, swept up, thrown away, consumed, and it shatters when it breaks.

You're a diamond, and you cannot break. The world cannot break you if you realize the value that God has placed on your life. This value must also come with a heightened self-worth and self love, just as we treat diamonds. Not everyone deserves you, is worth your attention, and can afford to be in your life. And you can't afford to leave your life, your body, your spirit, or your soul in the hands of just anyone. In six months, a year or two from now, I want to open an email or see a comment on Instagram from you sharing the fruit of your change. Include the hashtags #PoweroftheP #NoRing-NoTing). We'll all be celebrating with you! I can't wait.

I've said this a few times, and I'll say it a thousand more: I want you to experience the power of your P. This book is really my love letter to you. And I mean that. You mean so much to me and I want all of the blessings God is holding for you. I know it's possible for you to be blessed, in every area of your life. Many things are preventable, including heartbreak. When our minds and bodies remain pure—we are able to be an empty vessel for God to fill with the Holy Spirit.

Don't be the prey, be the catch

The sad truth is that most predators: liars, abusers, and manipulators scope out and select their prey very carefully. These predators choose their victims, often because of their posture. They seek out the weak, timid, and easily influenced. Hunters can smell when someone lacks the ability to protect themselves. When they do, they pounce. Domestic abusers often begin their cycle with emotional and verbal abuse to break down any resistance or mental strength of their victims. Molesters tell children that they hurt, "Don't tell anyone. This is our little secret." This is all a form of mind control that the physically stronger abuser uses to control their victims' bodies and minds and mold them into the perfect prey.

Mind-control tactics have been used since the beginning of time to orchestrate evil. Every battle is first a battle of the mind. That's why children should be taught the word of God and baptized in the Holy Spirit at a young age. This is partly why the Freeman tradition was that at age thirteen, my siblings and I took a purity pledge. As members of the body of Christ, we must cling closely to the Word of God so that we aren't able to be persuaded and manipulated. We need God's Word inside of us so we can pull it out and stand on its promises at all times. The Holy Spirit is absolutely vital. In 1 Thessalonians 2:13, it confirms this by saying that the Word works in those who believe. Believe and stand in God's Word. *But don't just listen to God's Word. You must do what it says. Otherwise, you are only fooling yourselves (James 1:22).* The stakes are just too high for you to not make God your highest priority. You demonstrate this and what you believe by living out His Word every day, or, on the other hand, choosing not to.

Catching The Flow of the Position

The Bible says, in ministry, we all have a position, as we are all a part of Christ's body. Some of us are the hands, some are the toes, and some are the feet. Some people are called to teach, preach, prophesy, be missionaries, or ministers. Regardless of what you do and who you were before you accepted Jesus as your savior, now you have a purpose and are a part of Christ's body. Romans 12:5 tells us, "So in Christ we, though many, form one body, and each member belongs to all the others." Find your position in God's kingdom. Find your purpose in God and be open to allow the Holy Spirit to move you and elevate you throughout your life. Once you're able to find that position in life, you'll notice that in different seasons and times, your posture and position will change, be it with jobs or marital status. However, God will never change. He will be your one constant. Always stand strong in what you believe and be willing to remain flexible to seasonal life changes.

I want to address any doubts that may be lingering in your mind about your purpose. I realize that only those who believe that they have a purpose in Christ and that He lives in you will be willing to make Him number one in your life. I know women who've been lost, and just like the scriptures say, now they are found.

They were blind (to Christ), but now they see. Once you are born again, you not only have God within you, but you also have Jesus and the Holy Spirit — the Holy Trinity— which is able to change your thoughts, actions, mind, and path, and to put you right back along the purpose that God predestined for you. And yes, everyone has a distinct purpose in Christ, even you. Let me show you:

Philippians 1:6 says, "He who began a good work in you will carry it on to completion until the day of Christ Jesus."

And, 1 Thessalonians 2:13 says, "...When you received the word of God which you heard from us, you accepted it not as the word of men, but for what it really is, the word of God, which also performs its work in you who believe."

Paul writes of his counterpart Peter in Galatians 2:8, "or He who effectually worked for Peter in his apostleship to the circumcised effectually worked for me also to the Gentile." (This demonstrates that God can and will work diligently in all those who love Him and are called according to His purpose (Romans 8:28)—YOU!)

So how do you activate God's "work in you" or His purpose and power in your life? You simply honor Him, trust Him, and live according to His word. Put Him in the top position! God works in us by making it possible for us to live by the spirit. Take a look at Galatians 5:16-17, "Walk by the Spirit, and you will not carry out the desire of the flesh. For the flesh sets its desire against the Spirit, and the Spirit against the flesh; for these are in opposition to one another, so that you may not do the things that you please."

The instructions are pretty clear here. We cannot do

80

what we (or our flesh wants to do). We have to be willing to be uncomfortable as we're being transformed, resting on the promise that God will not fail you and His Word will not come back void. You have to trust and believe that these scriptures didn't just apply to my life, my mom's life, your neighbor, or your friend who is seemingly living the *happily ever after* life. No. These words, God's Word, and promises of purpose apply to you as well. God's Word and His spirit are still very much alive today. You must realize that your fleshly desires are in direct opposition to the Holy Spirit, which lives inside of you. If you love God, you will honor Him, and live according to His Word—even though it's not comfortable at times.

So how will you honor God? How will you make Him number one? I want you to use the space below to write that out. Respond to a few questions that I thought about that may make your personal purpose and position very clear to you. But first, I want share a few stories from the Bible about people who believed God's promise and who followed their purpose.

As I am writing this, the Christmas season is upon us and, around the church, we often recount the various stories of Jesus and His birth. A few people in this story did something that I think was miraculous — they believed in God's promise, they went after it, (because faith without works is dead, right?), and finally, they allowed the Holy Spirit to speak to them. In doing so, they left the past behind.

These miraculous believers were the wise men, who are mentioned in Matthew 2:1-12. The story goes like this:

After Jesus was born in Bethlehem, wise men arrived in Jerusalem. They asked, "Where is the newborn king of the Jews? We saw his star as it rose, and we have come to worship him." They had faith in the prophesy, which had foretold

Jesus' birth. With that faith in God's promise, they traveled (outside of their comfort zone) to worship him in advance (not when they saw their promise come to fruition). After meeting with the King, they followed the star to Bethlehem, and it led them right to baby Jesus! After their mission was complete and they worshiped Him and adorned Him with gifts, they continued along their journey. God had spoken to them in a dream instructing them not to return to Jerusalem as the king had requested. They left the past where it was and continued along their path and God's purpose for them. Their posture and sole purpose was to honor the Lord and Savior Jesus Christ. They did not just read the scriptures and believe without taking action. Nope. These wise men put feet to their faith and made Christ their first priority.

How will you do this? What specific things can you do today to put God in the priority position in your life and become closer to Him?

How will you react if someone challenges your faith or decision to live for God? What can you do to remain in the spirit despite any challenges or setback?

What promises has God spoken to you? What is your purpose in the body of Christ?

What must you leave in the past to make it to God's future for you?

If you are unable to answer the questions regarding God's promise or purpose for your life, look back over the scriptures in this chapter and others that you may find, and apply God's best-case scenario to your passions and the things that you cannot stop thinking about. Once you are in the spirit and it resides in you, your passion will lead you to your purpose and God will continue to evolve it and make clear more parts of that purpose as you move along in life. Remember that all things work together for the good of those who are called according to God's purpose. That's you. So no more doubting your worth, future, or posture towards God. God's promise to you is that of an abundant future and an abundant life. Do you feel confident enough to welcome God into your favorite position yet?

For the mind set on the flesh is death, but the mind set on the Spirit is life and peace, because the mind set on the flesh is hostile toward God; for it does not subject itself to the law of God, for it is not even able to do so, and those who are in the flesh cannot please God.
However, you are not in the flesh but in the Spirit, if indeed the Spirit of God dwells in you. But if anyone does not have the Spirit of Christ, he does not belong to Him.
Romans 8:7-9

My Seventh Power Source: God is First in my Life
God is in the number one position in my life; therefore anything or anyone that competes with Him will have to go. I will not be distracted or lose my faith. Instead, I will believe and allow the Holy Spirit to dwell in me.

Purity Prayer
Dear Lord,
Thank you for saving me by grace and through the blood of Jesus. I understand that I can do all things through Christ who strengthens me. Please forgive me if I ever failed to put you first and make you the top priority in my life. Please fill me with your spirit, wisdom, guidance and discernment. Please make my path straight as I pursue your purpose for my life.
In Jesus' name I pray, Amen.

Purity Promise
Today, I leave all doubt behind, and I instead abide in God's word, under His care and with the Holy Spirit inside of me. Honoring God is my favorite position, and I will do that with my total heart, mind, body, and soul.

Chapter 8
Your Power over Soul Ties

For the word of God is alive and powerful. It is sharper than the sharpest two-edged sword, cutting between soul and spirit, between joint and marrow. It exposes our innermost thoughts and desires.
Hebrews 4:12

Sometimes life and love can get complicated. I wish I could say that Tim was my first and only relationship, but I can't. I dated a guy once that I was very fond of. He was amazing on so many levels and will be a great husband for some girl. However, there were things that I identified about our relationship that just weren't a good fit for me. What I mean is that even at that young age, I understood my assignment and purpose on this earth. I knew that whomever I decided to marry would need to complement that purpose, not complicate it.

So many people base their decisions to marry on how they feel, going just by their hearts. They fail to be logical and think. Our hearts and feelings are bound to change from day-to-day, but the truth, facts, and logic will remain the same. Our emotions are so out-of-whack sometimes, and before we know it, we're on what Vivian Green sang about—an *Emotional Rollercoaster*. Ever been there? If so, there's no doubt you too have experienced a negative soul tie. I talked a little about them in Chapter three, but I really want to dig deeper now.

Soul ties are deep emotional and spiritual bonds that connect you to another person. They tangle our hearts into one big ball of emotion, and if the soul tie is negative, a ball of confusion. Soul ties, while they can form outside of sex, are reinforced by sexual bonds. If you're having sex with someone, especially on a consistent basis, you have a soul tie with that person, and if and when they leave, you will feel a void — this is what a broken heart feels like. On the other hand, a positive soul tie is one developed through marriage. As the Bible says, a man should leave his father and mother and cling to his wife and the two will become one—this is a soul tie, a very positive one.

A married couple becomes in sync, closely connected, and can operate as one unit and achieve amazing things together. Soul ties have existed since the beginning of time. This is why Eve was able to persuade Adam to take a bite of that apple after she had been coerced by the devil. Soul ties are connections that run deep. Unless you are in a loving, committed relationship with someone who is on your purpose-path, you want to absolutely avoid soul ties. In the pages that follow, I'm going to give you some age-old wisdom about how to avoid them altogether and break those negative soul ties that may have you riding that Emotional Roller-coaster right now.

How to Avoid Soul Ties

Our hearts are emotionally unstable, which is why I would never advise you with a piece of bad advice that we hear so often, to just *go with your heart.* That's absolutely a wrong move. How many people do you know who have made decisions based on their hearts and have ended up dead, divorced, bitter, broken, and emotionally destroyed? The advice I'd give you instead would be to take note of how you feel, but most importantly, use your head.

My mom would always tell my siblings and me to never let a person you were interested in get inside of your head. She knew that if a person could get inside of your thoughts, they would also be able to get into your heart and influence how you make decisions. The first way to prevent getting involved in soul ties is to know and understand your purpose in life and to make decisions with your head and not your heart. Growing up, my dad always stressed the importance of thinking. He would just look at us and simply say, "All I want you to do is think." That same advice applies here. A wrong relationship could cloud your thinking and become pure clutter in your life. The right relationship will clear your thinking. It's that simple—black and white, with no shades of grey.

When you ignore the negative things that are going on in the beginning of a relationship, it will create a negative soul tie—and only negative results can stem from that. Setting standards in the beginning, as we've discussed earlier, is also a prevention mechanism. Remember that when you set the standards, do not break them. If someone tries to pressure you to compromise the standards you've set, this should automatically be a deal breaker for you. They do not or will not honor you and what you say you're about. To avoid entering negative soul ties, think with your head, set standards, never break them, and know your deal breakers. This is extremely important as you date and live in God's will for your life.

How to Break a Soul Tie
Soul ties can be easily broken when you apply the

principals of God's word. There are many scriptures to help with this process. For instance, Romans 12:2 states, "Don't copy the behavior and customs of this world, but let God transform you into a new person by changing the way you think. Then you will learn to know God's will for you, which is good and pleasing and perfect." When you want to move on from a relationship, it is crucial that you renew your mind.

This purging process of breaking soul ties works the same way as when a sinner leaves that life and becomes a Christian. When God says, "renew your mind," He understood that it would take a process of getting rid of our old ways that are contrary to His ways. Philippians 4:8 is another scripture where we are instructed exactly what to think, "And now, dear brothers and sisters, one final thing. Fix your thoughts on what is true, and honorable, and right, and pure, and lovely, and admirable. Think about things that are excellent and worthy of praise." Think of those positive things that will take you to a healthy and happy place.

My dad taught me that what I focus on will expand. This is something that I have to found to be so true. Have you ever wanted a new car, pair of shoes, or a nice bag, and right after you start wanting it, you start seeing it everywhere? It's not that these items suddenly became *so* popular after you found interest in them. They were always there. The only thing that changed was your focus. The moral of this story? Try not to meditate on how you feel, and instead start meditating on where your life is headed. Then you will begin to see that your focus will be moved away from the soul ties that you've developed. This forward focus will begin to manifest in your actions.

When you're leaving a relationship and breaking a soul tie, the most effective way to get over it in the flesh is to create ways to improve you. Go back to school or take a class—even if it's cooking lessons or dance class. Find ways to focus on you and it will be easier to move forward, but more importantly, you'll begin to feel great about yourself again. When you focus on improving you and get involved in new things, you will rebuild your confidence and independence. This is key in breaking soul ties and mending your heart.

Start Now

If you're in a relationship where there's a soul tie—there's likely some other things working below the surface such as codependency. Codependency is when two people rely heavily on each other—sometimes in unhealthy ways. Even when they both know they aren't right for each other, it becomes hard to leave. Codependent relationships can be extremely unhealthy and hinder every area of your life. It's important that you start the process of breaking this tie now, because your future literally depends on it.

Denounce the soul tie(s) in your life. Repent from any sins you've committed while in this relationship and develop a plan to stay "clean." Yes you must develop a plan to stay pure, just like drug and alcohol addicts do. That's exactly the effect of a soul tie—it becomes an addictive drug that sucks you in, consumes you in sin, and separates you from God. If you're in a negative soul tie, you are out of God's will for your life—a place where you cannot possibly be blessed for an extended amount of time. Break free and start now!

My Eighth Power Source: Strength over Soul Ties

Now that I am aware of the dangers of soul ties, and I have the power to avoid them, I will remain focused on my journey and withstand any attempts by anyone to manipulate my emotions.

Purity Prayer

Dear Lord,

Thank you for giving me the power to break free and avoid negative soul ties. I repent from the sins that I've committed while under the control of them. Please continue to show me grace and guidance as I keep my heart and thoughts on you.
In Jesus' name, Amen.

Purity Promise

Today I promise to guard my heart and my thoughts, to make logical decisions based on clear thinking, and to pray for discernment in my relationships.

Chapter 9
Save Yourself, Don't Protect Yourself

For this is the will of God, your sanctification: that you abstain from sexual immorality; that each one of you know how to control his own body in holiness and honor,
1 Thessalonians 4:3-4

The world teaches us to protect ourselves. When you were younger, perhaps you had a talk with your parents about the "birds and the bees." Maybe they didn't discourage you. They may have even said, "If you do it, this is how you protect yourself. I don't want any more kids in my house." I don't blame parents. This is all they knew, and to be honest it's what their parents taught them, because it's what they knew. These lowered expectations of children have been passed down from generation to generation. Oftentimes, because our elders had children early or had sex early, kids are taught to believe that saving themselves altogether isn't even an option. Think of it this way: If I told you that for lunch you could have chicken or you could have steak, and I never mentioned that there was a veggie plate inside of the refrigerator that was another option for lunch, you'd most likely choose the chicken or the steak, simply because those were the only two options laid before you.

For too long, parents have taught children that the only options concerning sex was to have sex with no protection at all or to have sex with protection and reducing the rates of unwanted pregnancies and STDs. Many children and teenagers who are growing up in a sexually infused world never even considered "no sex" as an option. Not enough parents included conversations about exalting God's promise over pressure and abstaining from sex until marriage—because the Bible says so. I'm of the belief that if you teach a child the way they should go, and provide clear examples for that lifestyle, they will indeed follow that teaching—with a little reinforcement.

So society altogether has lowered the expectations around sex. Schools, social services organizations, and big highway billboards promoting safe sex and "Wrap it up," don't drive home the point or raise our conscious to the ultimate truth—the only way to protect yourself is to save yourself. You're heard the saying, "When you know better, you do better." Well now that you know, no one is to blame for your decision to have sex (or not) except you. You know.

The Bible teaches us to abstain from sex before marriage. Since we *do* believe and we also *do* the Bible, this is what we should teach our kids. We would not only reduce the STD rate, but eliminate it altogether, by just by abstaining having sex. If you're out having sex with any Joe Blow, chances are you'll end up with what the last girl had. Most men won't tell you if the last girl he was with caught something.

If you don't want anything from anyone, why allow yourself to get caught up in a moment, a moment that could cost a lifetime? We have to stop being moment thinkers and become lifetime thinkers instead. Like my dad always says,

"Just think." While eliminating the risks of STDs is a huge reason why "save yourself" should be taught over "protect yourself," that's not the only reason, of course. Saving yourself is an overall great strategy for managing many stresses and issues that come up in life.

Sometimes, it takes imagining the end result of certain things for us to increase our self-control. If we know the end result of our actions, many times, we wouldn't do certain things. I know for me, I couldn't have sex. My name would've been all over Washington D.C. My parents would've been disappointed and my entire family would have been as well. So I had to take my mind to the end result just to walk away from a heated situation. If you put the moment of pleasure over the lifetime of frustration, you will rarely make a level-headed decision. Instead, you'll be moved by any old thing that arouses your emotions or turns you on. Remember to always exalt the promise over the pressure.

This simple mind exercise will not only help with maintaining your purity, but with your self-control all together. Imagine the results of reacting physically to a heated argument, responding to road rage, or saying the first thing that comes to your head during when you disagree with something someone says. Naturally, as women, we are emotional and we love to be loved. We love to be included and we loved to be held. It's just a normal thing, but I have good news. We're in control of all of our emotions and we have the power! You aren't powerless! Embrace the power of your P. Forget the "Third Date Rule", and the "30 Day or 60 Day Rule"—none of them apply to you. You're above that. If you're reading this, you are living by the "I'm Waiting Until I'm Married Rule."

Let's raise the bar again. Erase the faulty teaching you've lived by thus far. You don't have to have sex. Protect ing yourself doesn't just mean using condoms. The only way to protect yourself is to save yourself. You are also worth more than some silly social dating rule, meaning you don't have to adhere to someone else's guidelines when it comes to sex. If it's in your heart to follow God's Word, you can be abstinent, still date, and remove the worries associated with that part of a relationship. Let's make men have to work for us again. Let's stop being pressed and scared that we'll lose something good if we don't have sex. Perhaps you aren't afraid to lose a man, but you are an independent woman who simply likes sex. You're used to being free and in total control of your body, and when you want it, you simply go for it.

Maybe you even seduce men, and you know that once they have sex with you, they'll fall at your feet and will *want to* marry you. No matter which side of the spectrum you fall, and even if sex for you isn't a matter of being pressed or behaving desperately, you are still being weak to your flesh if you simply have sex because you want to. You can demonstrate much more mental and emotional strength by putting aside your own wants, and instead, going after what God wants for you. What could you lose by doing things God's way for once? If you've never been married, or you've been divorced and are looking to remarry, what would it hurt for you to activate the power of your P, and see what results you get by exalting God's promise?

If you love your man enough to give your body to him, can you wait to find out if he loves you first? Are you meant to be together? If the answers are yes, why not build a strong relationship and explore the option of being married? Why are you giving men who aren't worth your life access to your life through your body? I just want you to think about that for a minute, okay? I promise you, if he can't wait, he's not even worth the wait. If a man doesn't have the patience or the respect to honor you, he's not good for you.

Saving yourself is the only 100 percent guaranteed way to protect yourself—from a number of things. When the world talks about protecting yourself, it doesn't share all of the things that just protecting yourself with a condom will fail to save you from. Having the attitude, *I can have sex as long as I protect myself,* is dangerous. No birth control can protect your heart, your mind, your spirit, your time, your salvation, and your promise from God. What if you decide to have sex and to simply protect yourself, the condom pops, or it feels strange and the guy you're with just chooses to remove it? You're in the heat of the moment, and you've already committed to having sex in the first place—what will you do? Save yourself the heartache, frustration, feelings of regret, and potential soul ties by living your life according to the Word of God.

Let's discuss another myth that many Christians believe: Lust will go away after marriage. I've heard so many people say and share their beliefs that the struggle with sexual lust will just disappear after they get married, once they're "getting some" on a regular basis, or they have a live-in sex partner. This is not true! Lust is a spirit, and if you don't deal with it before marriage, you'll still have to deal with it in marriage. I'm from the DC area, and where I live the social scene is often driven by nightclubs and Instagram. You can see so much lust play out in both of these atmospheres.

The lust that leads to unfaithfulness in a relationship prior to marriage will lead to adultery within a marriage. The lust that entices people to watch pornography, sext, and send nudes before marriage, will lead to the same behavior (and oftentimes in the form of an affair) once two people are married. Giving into lust simply sets a microwave mentality with sex—having your arousals pleased immediately. Regularly giving into lust will also lead to boredom and never being completely satisfied. Once your lust has been fulfilled—and even in marriage—you'll become bored and your flesh will desire more. It's like a drug. When a fiend has used their drug of pleasure enough, they develop a level of tolerance. So they need more and more to reach that ultimate high they felt the first time they tried it.

Just think historically to the War on Drugs and the crack epidemic that took over inner city streets during the '80s and '90s. Crack became so dangerous because it gave users such a high and an initial pleasure that they began to crave it more and more, and as they became addicted, the drug didn't have its same effect. So they required more. The more drug they needed, the more of themselves, along with their belongings, homes, money, and family, they were willing to give up just to feel that high again. Lust is the same way. It will pop up in areas of fornication, porn, or in sexually impure things you want your spouses to do if you're not careful. This is why I preach that purity is not just about having a "virginity" or "protecting yourself" mindset. It's more of a mindset to carry through life. When I say save yourself and not protect yourself, I'm urging you to save your life from the wicked dangers of this world.

I know I've raised the bar here and am asking you to take more responsibilities for your thoughts and actions. I know there's someone reading this who is rethinking their behaviors and beliefs all together. This is good. This book is about self-conviction, not condemnation—the same self-conviction that every Christian has when we're up to no good or living unGodly.

I truly love those wristbands and memes that ask us, "What would Jesus do?" or "WWJD?" That simple question causes us to truly take a step back from our own fleshly de sires, to step back from the evils of the world, the seduction, manipulation, and self-gratifying behavior we can become consumed with and instead become self-aware. This is a good thing. Asking ourselves, *WWJD?* is like a guiding light—a GPS to righteous living. We know despite suffering through persecution, Jesus never sinned, not once. So as you consider your own rules for sex and dating, ask yourself what would Jesus do? Would He save himself, or would He protect himself? Would Jesus believe that the only way to protect himself is to save himself?

I mentioned social media in my city and how it heavily influences the social scene here. One of the most common relationship cycles I notice is breakups. Whenever a relationship ends, the women often scrubs her Instagram of all the photos and memories of her and the guy she broke up with. It's not uncommon to see this same cycle play out with the same woman two to three times a year. I'm not judging, but I do pray and hope that these will simply heal and save themselves from the reoccurring breakup process. See the thing is, if you're still healing from the last relationship, you shouldn't be dating. You should instead be waiting and growing closer to God. Because of how relationships often play out on social media, I believe that many women and men, for that matter, failed to date with purpose and set the standards we discussed in the purpose-driven dating chapter. Again, if you're not dating with purpose, you're dating for your own personal pleasures and your dating life is not sustainable.

Many women believe that having sex with a man automatically means commitment and consistency in a relationship. This, again, is faulty thinking. What you're doing instead is fulfilling his fleshly desires—his lust and your own. If you're questioning my thinking, just think about how many beautiful women you know in committed relationships—even marriages—with men who cheat on them with women who aren't as pretty and have less to offer. This man has an issue with lust and sexual impurity that his wife didn't realize prior to the marriage. Why did she overlook it? She didn't put the promise over the pleasure. She was likely the person fulfilling his lust. It was still new and nothing permanent. But see, the married life brings things into focus—your life and relationship suddenly seems like forever. People who have not dealt with their sexual lust will try doing it just to see if they can get away with it, and then fall into Pandora's box of sexual immorality.

One of the most important thoughts I can leave with you, especially if you're still single, is that saving yourself right now can protect you from a lifestyle that you don't want and are not ready for. In marriage, there are no breaks, and you have to think twice before leaving. You can't bail out or run when there's an argument or something gets hard. For most married people, divorce is seriously the last option. Many people who fail to date with due diligence and truly learn their partner, including their habits and potential issues like lust, get married. So what happens next? They cannot protect themselves from what is guaranteed to come down the pike.

Their marriages are turned upside down as people become more comfortable in marriage and their true, unfiltered selves begin to show up, which can take years to happen. When you date with purpose and without sex being involved, you can truly see where someone's head is at, how patient they are, and you'll learn their fleshly desires. You'll get to decide, without the emotional weight of sex, whether or not you can deal with those things in marriage. You will also protect yourself from getting into a situation that's not for you. There are so many women who were pressed for their men, pressed to get married, and now they have their wish. Yes, they have the marriage and the ring, but they are also forced to deal with infidelity, a wondering eye, insincerity, and thoughtlessness from their husbands. Why? Because this is the behavior their dating led them to. And this was the behavior that was there all along, but it was overlooked. These women have made a lifelong commitment to God, so now they have to settle in their marriage and for a less-than-fairytale lifestyle. I don't want this for you.

Instead of becoming one of these women who are stuck with the question, "Why me?" save yourself and protect yourself by keeping your eye on God's promise. You have the control and power over all lust, and you can have a fulfilled and fun life—and even a dating life—without having sex. There are so many things to do without sex, and you will protect your head, heart, and future by abstaining. Trust me.

My Ninth Power Source - Saving Myself is How I Will Protect Myself

I do not have to adhere to social dating standards or rules for when to have sex. The only rule I live by is that I'm saving myself until marriage.

Purity Prayer

Dear Lord,

Thank you for wisdom, knowledge, and discernment. I pray that you continue to pour these virtues into me as I continue to save myself in order to protect my heart, mind, and soul from the negative consequences of sex before marriage. In Jesus' name I pray, Amen.

Purity Promise

Today, I promise myself that I will no longer look at "protecting myself" as the proper way to go about sex. I understand that saving myself is the only protection against the consequences of premarital sex.

Chapter 10

Answered Prayers

And whatever we ask we receive from him, because we keep
his commandments and do what pleases him.
1 John 3:22

Growing up, I had this prayer list that described my ideal husband. I wanted a virgin, a man of God, someone who loved God and loved me. I wanted to be with a singer, and he could be any complexion. Basically that was the gist of my list. It's funny when I look back at it. When I was a teenager, I told my father, "Dad I want to marry a virgin," and he literally laughed. He said the chances of that were slim to none. I understood why—sex is just a part of life, and the older we get, virgins are very rare. Still, that's what I wanted. In my mind, when I thought about getting married, I thought, *Why can't I have someone who is saving himself, if I'm saving myself?*

I knew I couldn't pray for things that were against the will of God, and so I felt my prayers had to be answered, because they were in line with God's Word. Now I know I'm a bit extreme, and sometimes you have to be realistic. If you're knocking fifty years old, and you're looking to marry or remarry, the chances that you both will be virgins are rare. But if you've lived your life by certain standards and biblical principles, according to God's Word, you can stand on that. You can declare and claim those things for your life. Since I had honored God, I had confidence to go to Him and ask for what I wanted. I knew He'd answer my prayers.

As a teenager, I dated other guys who weren't virgins. When I met Tim Bowman, we clicked. We both absolutely love church and God, and he was a virgin, too. He was also a singer (did God do it or what?). The day he proposed to me, my prayers were literally answered. When we got engaged, we became even stronger together, because God was the center of both of our lives. Tim and I truly experienced favor in our journey throughout our engagement (I talk more about this in later in the book). This favor has made us relentless in asking for what we want through prayer and trusting God through faith.

My prayer life is no joke, and I believe and trust in God wholeheartedly. I trust that He will answer my prayers because I know that He honors His Word. I also don't play when it comes to honoring God when He answers one of my prayers. I've noticed that a lot of people take their blessings and answered prayers for granted. Or they label their blessings as luck and attribute them to people. This is what sets believers who live extraordinary lives through faith apart from those who live regular lives. When your prayers are answered, declare, "I believed God for this, and God provided." God often blesses us through people. So when you've prayed for something and that blessing comes to you through someone else, realize that God is at work. Once you start to attribute your blessings to God, you'll start becoming more confident that your prayers will be answered. You'll find yourself in the faith process, where you start asking and believing God for stuff. He'll deliver, and when he does, you need to be a living witness. This is not only my story, but the story of many. In the Bible, over and over, we see stories play out with people who have declared their blessings and gifts as works of God or works for God, and He delivered for them. In 1 Samuel, Hannah's story illustrates this.

For years, Hannah was unable to have children, and her husband's second wife would taunt her for that. One day, Hannah was so distraught that she prayed to the Lord and asked Him to give her a child, and she promised that child's life would be dedicated to the Lord. A few years later, God delivered for Hannah, and Hannah kept good on her promise. She also attributed that blessing as an answered prayer from God.

No Mediocre

Many Christians who haven't developed a strong prayer life and who only go to God when they are in trouble, claim to have faith, but they only activate that faith during times of need. I've learned that God doesn't want us to be basic, mediocre, or to struggle. Will we face hard times? Yes. Are Christians persecuted? Yes. Jesus was, and we will be, too. But this takes nothing away from passages in the Bible that declare God's desire for us to have an abundant life. When you start praying and getting into a relationship with God, the desires of your heart will become in sync with God's desires for your life. Because God loves you and you love God, you should start believing God for the desires of your heart. He wants to take care of you, and He wants you to live a good life. So far this book has been a build up to the final chapters—the payoff of living a life that honors God completely. If you're really ready to unleash the power of your P, you have to truly go big in terms of prayer, and believe God for the big things—you need to have big faith, not mediocre faith.

But realize there is a prerequisite for reaping the blessings of God and living a truly blessed life. Please don't make the mistake and pick and choose which parts of the Bible you'll believe and follow. If you're a Christian, you should be serious in your walk. Get serious about your journey, because when you do, God will get serious about exposing you to some stuff that will blow your mind. I've come to realize that when our minds and bodies are pure, and we're constantly abiding in God's Word, we can expect and ask for certain things from God. That's right, your prayers will be answered, again and again.

Imagine this familiar scenario: There's a girl name Sophie who is a great student. Sophie's parents told her that if she did well in school and made the Honor Roll, she'd get a special treat. She also knew that her payoff for good behavior—the time spent studying and excelling in her work—would result in recognition from the school and her peers. Just like Sophie will grow to expect certain rewards for her good behavior and performance, you can expect the same thing from God for yours. So just like it was with school, show up for God every day, on time—have perfect attendance. Work for Him day in and out. When He gives you a test, think *WWJD?—or BETTER YET, what does God want me to do?* Then, do your best.

If you're dedicated to your walk with God and honoring Him, as much as He's dedicated to elevating you in each season toward your promise, just as you were elevated from grade to grade after passing enough tests and showing up for enough days every year, you can pray with expectation that God will move you to the next level toward your promise. You no longer have to be a struggle Christian—one who is always begging God to deliver you from the world's evils or save you after you've messed up. I'm not implying or saying that you won't still need God for these things. What I am saying is that when you begin to abide with Him 24/7, your thoughts and actions will become more like His, and you can start raising the stakes on your prayer life—your blessed life.

God is more than a rescuer and He's made you more than a conqueror. You are not basic, mediocre, or average. God doesn't even want you to be. There's no need to be a small-minded Christian, believing God to come through on just the little things (or every once in a while on the big things) while you hope and wish for something major to happen for you. At this point in your walk, I want you to start dreaming and praying big. Start asking God for stuff within His will that you desire. One of my answered prayers, concerning Tim, is to be able to support his dream. I wanted to marry someone whose vision and dreams I could be a part of and vice versa.

I didn't want to have to create a life on my end and him create a life on his end, without synergies. Being Mrs. Bowman has been the best time of my life, and it's more special because I'm able to support my husband to achieve the success he seeks and to live out the purpose God has for him. His song, "I'm Good", is currently climbing the Billboard Charts and it's up for a few gospel music awards. It feels great to be a part of it, to attend studio sessions, performances, and to watch him work. Similarly, he really enjoyed helping me with this book and hearing my ideas for the future. We are truly one.

Writing this book and speaking to you through these pages was another big dream and is now an answered prayer of mine. I want you to really think about your big dreams. What's on your heart? What you are praying and believing God for, or what would pray and believe for if you knew He would deliver it? You should dream big and pray big. If your dreams and prayers are within God's will, take it a step further and demand and declare them for your life. Luke 11:9 says, "Ask and it will be given to you; seek and you will find; knock and the door will be opened to you." Why are so many Christians living small and praying small when God has predestined a wonderful life for us all? A part of my purpose is to expose people to the other side of purity. I believe that we need to start trusting and having faith in God more, not just for our needs, but the desires of our hearts. If we're honoring Him, we can expect big things in return.

What I love about being in God and God being in us is that as we start to pray more, He starts to download His desires for us into our hearts. Throughout my life, I just wanted to honor God, and I always thought I wanted my husband to be a virgin, simply because that was my desire. But the entire time, God had it planned out. This was really His desire, so that our lives could bless others and ultimately give honor to Him. It wasn't about me. Together, Tim and I have been able to help so many people. Boys come up to him all of the time to tell him how inspired they are by his story and the fact that he was a virgin when he got married. Our marriage and our lives are impacting people we don't even know yet, and it's been amazing to see God working through us. It's a testament to how critical it is to put Him first and to honor Him in everything you do.

Living a life of purity is more than just saving yourself or being a virgin. It's about honoring God so that you can experience the fullness of life. Tim and I were able to have the honeymoon of our dreams and live an amazing lifestyle. Through the way we live, we can demonstrate that it's a lot more to life than work, church, going to eat, and coming home. You only believe God for the things that you're exposed to. If nobody ever told you that it's possible to have the good life, then you won't even know that it's possible. I'm here to tell you that it's possible, and it's waiting for you.

If you're honoring God, ask yourself honestly, *What's my ultimate goal?* Is your ultimate goal to be married or is it to please God? What if your ministry is to be single? What if that's your purpose? My answered prayers weren't just about being married, they were, and still are, more about being fulfilled. There are a lot of married people who wish they were single, and on the flip, there are plenty of single people who want to be married. Somebody has a choice. You have an option while you're single. You need to take every look and uncover every desire and purpose for your life. When you're single, you have so many things to explore, goals to achieve, and a chance to become whoever you want, and now is the time to discover them. If you don't know that, when you get in a relationship, you'll lose yourself. One thing I love about Tim is that we are both so secure in who we are and we spent time figuring ourselves and our lives out before we were married. Now we can build and we don't have to discover ourselves as we go along.

When you live in purity, you can fully focus on yourself and who God created you to be. You can learn who you are before you get married and find your purpose in love. This is so important; when you get with someone who is ready to go, you better be ready to move. I'm speaking in terms of faith now. I have huge faith, and I couldn't imagine being with someone whose faith was at a smaller level. We wouldn't be in build mode as a couple. I'd be ready to build and my husband would still be searching. It would take me some time to get him to believe that God can do what He says that He can do. If I'm believing God for a mansion and he wanted a two-bedroom apartment, it would be really tough. Do you see where I'm going here?

Don't be so desperate to be with someone or to be married that you fail to discover or lose all of who you are in the process. Before I had my store, I remember being with this guy. I wanted to be with him so much that his dream became my dream and I lost so much of myself before I finally realized it. I had let all of my desires go, and instead, I had convinced myself that I was going to be a stay-at-home mom, because he wanted that. I was even willing to move to where he wanted to go. One day I stepped back and asked myself, *"Is this what I want? You like to work, in fact, you're a workaholic."* There's nothing wrong with being a stay-at-home mom, but it wasn't my dream. When I realized that I had started to create this false reality of what I wanted, I had to step back and tell myself that keeping a relationship wasn't worth losing me. I needed my own life and I had my own dreams.

Not going after your dreams is just like having a list at the beginning of the day of things you want to accomplish, however at the end of your day, you realize you didn't get anything done on that list. Now imagine if that was your life. In that relationship, I decided to keep myself first. I told my boyfriend, "No, here's what I want. Either you can handle it or you can't." When you are single you have that option—to seek and find who you are. Don't be so eager to be in a relationship that you've failed to write your own list of the desires you want for your life. If you do, you'll wake up one day and realize that you supported him along the way, but you didn't really fulfill the desires of your heart.

Going through that process with my ex changed my heart. It made me realize that I never want to be in a place where I have to settle. After that, I started to truly figure out what I wanted, and I prayed for those desires and went after them, relentlessly. I took a look in the mirror and worked on my mind. It was hard, but I knew I had to do it to get clear again on who I was and what I wanted.

We don't like to look in the mirror at our own issues. When we do, we feel less than. But, I challenge you to think and answer the question: If I can become better, what is it that I can do?

Too often, people will jump from relationship to relationship, simply because they want to be with someone. They will spend two months with "John" and five months with "Andrew," and never take time alone—searching the desires of their hearts and praying for God to reveal those things. You are wasting valuable time when you spend a few months with this person, and another few months with that person. It would be so much easier, and more efficient, to just search within, figure out who you are, and start walking in your purpose. If you're hurting, you shouldn't be dating. You should be praying and allowing God to heal you.

It's never too late or too early to figure out your purpose. When we become purpose and promise-driven, our journey becomes more consistent. This comes naturally, because now we are moving with our promise in mind. With God's spirit inside of us, we aren't so easily distracted. If we can stay consistent throughout the whole journey, we'll notice lives begin to change. It's just like working out—it gets harder and harder, but if you can just stay in there and complete the process, over time, it will get easier. After so many months of dedication, your consistency will become a lifestyle and, simply, what you do.

People ask me all the time if it would have been a deal breaker for me if Tim has not been a virgin. Surprising to some, my answer is no. Tim wasn't my only answered prayer. God has been blessing me and providing me with the desires of my heart all throughout my life. I honored Him and He gave me vision to do certain things as a reward. My desires became synchronized with His. What I really want you to understand is that God has predestined our lives to work out. I am after the fulfilled life, so I pray and put my promise first. I wanted a worry-free life, one filled with family, love, ministry, business, travel, and luxury. (I am not ashamed to say I love the finer things, and you shouldn't either).

If all of your needs were taken care of, would you really be stressed out? No. So today, I want you to think about the questions below and write down your answers. If your prayers are going to be answered, we need to figure out what you're praying for and what you are trusting God to provide, as well as how you pray. I want you to start declaring blessings over your life.

How often do you pray?

What are you trusting God for and praying for in your personal life, professional life, and spiritual life?
(Remember you cannot pray for things that are not within the will of God and expect them to come to past.)

What does a fulfilled life look like to you?

What can you begin praying for so that you will be fulfilled?

Are you on the path of doing everything you want in life? If no, what needs to change today?

My Tenth Power Source - Answered Prayers

God has proved that He can and will provide all my needs.
I'm trusting Him to download desires into my heart and answer my prayers in line with His Word and will.

Purity Prayer

Dear Lord,
Thank you for predesigning my life to work out for my good.
I pray for a fulfilled life, a blessed life, and to experience the
best that you have to offer for me both here on earth and in
heaven. I no longer want to live or be a mediocre Christian.
I'm trusting you to answer my big prayers—and I'm leaning
on you to provide my needs and also my desires.
In your Holy Name I pray, Amen.

Purity Promise

Today, I promise to begin praying intentional prayers and
speaking blessings over my life. I promise to seek God more
and more daily, so that my desires can become in sync with
His desires for my life.

Chapter

Favor in your Journey

For you bless the righteous, O Lord; you cover him with
favor as with a shield.
Psalm 5:12

Fast forward to my engagement, December 25, 2014. I decided immediately that I was going to have a big wedding. Tim knows everyone, and with my father being who he is, I knew it would be a lot of people. After I got engaged, I read a book about a woman who was also engaged to be married. She and her fiancé were truly honoring God with their lives, and she wrote about how people literally just started blessing them with all types of things throughout their engagement. So as I read this book, I literally put a demand on my life for the blessings and favor that she had received. I told myself, *If she could have these blessings, I can have them, too.*

I started speaking abundant blessings over our wedding. I even told my mom, "I am believing God for $70,000 for this entire wedding and honeymoon." I started placing a demand on what I had been believing in for years. God heard me and He answered—money literally started coming in the mail like crazy. I never knew where it would come from or how it would come. People would send me checks or see me and give me money, telling me that God instructed them to

113

sow a seed into my life.

A lady I didn't know sowed a thousand dollars toward my wedding dress. Someone else paid for our wedding cocktail reception. Normally, 500 invitations would have cost between $2,500 and $3,500. I literally paid $300 for all of my invitations! Gifts poured in left and right, and favor from every direction. Once we even went to Bed, Bath & Beyond, and the cashier gave us 50% discount off our purchase. After we used all the gift cards we'd received, our $800 bill came to just $20.

Even down to our honeymoon in the Jumeirah Emirates Towers in Dubai, which sits on a beautiful island right in the Indian Ocean, we were blessed. Our total trip cost about $11,000. For our honeymoon alone we received $5,000, and this seed came before the wedding. If you could imagine how it felt to receive that kind of gift prior to the wedding reception—we were stunned. We know without a shadow of a doubt that what we're doing is right and nobody can doubt it just based on the overflow of blessings and abundance in our lives.

While we are blessed through people, we have to be sure to give honor where it's due, and that's to God. Sometimes, when we sow into people's lives, we expect the harvest to come from them. What we often don't realize is that the harvest can come from anywhere. We shouldn't expect anyone to return things we've given to them, because in actuality we are blessing them, but honoring God. (Remember that all things work together for the good of those who love the Lord and are called according to His purpose.) So God will, in turn, provide a harvest back to us, and it will often come in the form of another person who decides to sow into our lives. This was the case with Tim and me. People were sowing into our lives left and right, and I'm never in a place where I'm settled or unappreciative of what God is doing. I'm always in shock and belief. I've become dependent on this faith process where I speak things for my life, pray, and trust God for them, and He provides.

Still, every time it blows my mind—it's a surprise and always better than I had imagined. After all He's done, how can I not believe God for the things that I know I can have? I tell you this to say that there will be favor in your journey as well. God is not new, He doesn't change, and what He does for one person, He *will* do for the next one as well. He wants us to have faith and believe the wonderful promises of the Bible and the amazing promises that He's placed over our lives. I know for sure that because Tim and I believe and we live like we believe, we've experienced unfathomable favor in every aspect of our journey.

We've been consistent in our walk with Christ, and so His blessings and favor have been consistent in our lives. I want this to be your testimony and the testimony of all who believe in God. I want you to activate the power of your P through consistent, righteous living. God has called us to be better than mediocre. Our consistent journeys of faith will garner our Lord's consistent favor.

My son, do not forget my teaching, but let your heart keep my commandments, for length of days and years of life and peace they will add to you. Let not steadfast love and faithfulness forsake you; bind them around your neck; write them on the tablet of your heart. So you will find favor and good success in the sight of God and man.
Proverbs 3:1-4

You will find favor and good success in the sight of God and man....

God knew the desires of our hearts. Although we wanted a dream wedding, we also didn't want our wedding bills to go with us to the honeymoon, and we didn't want our honeymoon bills to go with us into our new home. The favor we received could have only been God-sent. I believe we activated His favor through our faith and obedience to His word. We knew that He could provide and that He'd bless us, because our union was in His will, and our lives honored Him. But we also knew that we could activate favor in our journey through obedience to God's will.

This favor is not just set aside for certain people. While the promises of God can be viewed as exclusive, these promises are also inclusive, and divine favor belongs to the children of Christ. To activate it, you must truly believe that Jesus is Lord, have faith in God's word and promise for your life and be obedient to His word. You must also realize that what you sow you will reap, and live a life that uplifts God's kingdom.

Remember I said that your work and life can't be about you and you alone? This is because God blesses things that bless others and gives glory to Him. We talked so much about finding your purpose in God earlier in this book, because once you do, you'll find that this purpose isn't just about you. It's not about getting rich or being blessed alone. Once you find God's purpose for your life, you enter the journey toward your promise, and everything becomes about honoring God.

Even with Tim's song, "I'm Good," a lady woke up one day who wanted to commit suicide, she heard Tim's song and she literally decided not to take her life. God's favor over Tim's ministry enabled his gift to save a life. But this isn't about Tim—it's about God. You have a life-saving ministry inside of you, and once you begin to activate the power of your P, God will show you so much favor. Like Tim, what you're doing isn't about you. Your righteous life is honoring God and supporting God's kingdom. To honor God, you honor His children and give to His children. It's a cycle in a sense. If everyone is walking in their purpose, we're all giving to the kingdom, and God finds ways to bless His children and provide favor for our journeys.

Give, and you will receive. Your gift will return to you in full—pressed down, shaken together to make room for more, running over, and poured into your lap. The amount you give will determine the amount you get back."
Luke 6:38 (NLT)

Divine favor is reserved exclusively for those who live according to God's word. This is why I believe that having a purity mindset and living a life of purity is the quickest road to the glory and riches of God. When we are pure in mind, body and spirit, God's thoughts become our thoughts, His desires become our desires, and His will becomes our will. It's a lifestyle that's not just about being a virgin or abstaining from sex, but one about true purity so that we can become injected with the Holy Spirit. If I had placed my life and worth on the fact that I was a virgin, I would've lost my entire identity when I got married and was no longer a virgin. It's bigger than virginity and sexual purity. Becoming pure, in mind, body, and spirit creates a level of Christ-centered discipline that transcends every part of our lives.

Favor is reserved for the righteous. Favor is reserved for those who are obedient to God's Word and who live a life that honors Him. Your righteous living will result in favor in your journey—no matter if your road is tough and you're battling the devil in this season, if you're a missionary spreading the good news of Jesus, or if you're engaged to be married and are praying for blessings along the way. God's favor is with you.

Favor in your Journey is a Promise from God

God has promised you favor. Do you believe this now? Are you confident that you too have inherited a great destiny with favor from God? No matter where you are in your journey, if you simply keep your faith and wear it like a badge of honor, God will protect you. There are countless examples from people—both modern-day and from the bible—that we can use as proof to us that God shows His children favor: Job, Jacob, Abraham, Moses, Paul, Peter, Esther, David, Jesus.... the stories are endless. We should be inspired by those who had great faith, even during adversity, or when they were underrated, overlooked, mistreated, forgotten, nearly dead, or quite successful—the stories of God's favor for those who love Him are endless. Favor is what He's promised to us, as His children.

One of my favorite people of the Bible is David who wrote in Psalm 34:10, "Those who seek the Lord lack no good thing." His life proved this over and over again. From the very beginning, David experienced God's favor. In 1 Samuel 16, the prophet Samuel was looking for guidance on who would be the next king of Israel. The new king was destined to be one of Jesse's sons. So all of his sons appeared before Samuel. But they didn't meet the cut—God was not satisfied with David's brothers.

The Lord had not predestined any of the other sons to take the seat of king. That's when Samuel learned of David, who was in the field tending to his father's sheep, and who everyone had counted out as the future king. While David didn't have his brothers' credentials, what he did have was God's favor. Why? Because he honored God. Acts 13:22

reads, "But God removed Saul and replaced him with David, a man about whom God said, 'I have found David son of Jesse, a man after my own heart. He will do everything I want him to do.'

See, God wants to be able to use us. Our life doesn't belong to us. It belongs to God, which is why if we seek Him, we will find Him. God is already in us. We please Him when we live as representatives for Him, and our lives need to be righteous both in church and outside of church. I remember being in Los Angeles, 3,000 miles away from home. I got a call from my mom that someone had seen Tim and me out eating breakfast. She told my mom that we "were so cute." I remember this day clearly, because I had just threw on some sweatpants to grab a bite to eat. One person saw me, who texted her sister. That person called my mom, who then called me. What if my life was just a show and I didn't actually live to honor God? Or what if Tim had been yelling at me or cursing me out? That same lady would've called her sister who would've called my mother and God knows who else, and news would've soon spread. See what I mean?

As believers, we are always representing Christ, and someone is always watching. We have been called to spread the gospel throughout the earth. You might be the only version of Jesus that someone sees. What type of representation will you be? How will you spread the gospel?

To experience favor in our journey beyond what we believe or can imagine, there are certain principles that we must live by and behaviors that we must follow daily.

Operate in your faith.

Matthew 6:31-33 says, "Therefore do not be anxious, saying, 'What shall we eat?' or 'What shall we drink?' or 'What shall we wear?' For the Gentiles seek after all these things, and your heavenly Father knows that you need them all. But seek first the kingdom of God and his righteousness, and all these things will be added to you." **Seek first the kingdom of God…**

We are directed to operate in our faith in all situations, because God knows our needs and will provide.

Our faith is exercised when we're faced with fear—when situations look dim—when we're waiting on the promises of God, *(and sometimes He keeps us waiting longer than we would like).* No matter our situation or what we're faced with we are to have faith. Our faith is in God and in His word. I began to speak blessings over my life, and I refused to be mediocre, because I had faith in God and in scripture. God has taken care of my needs, and now I speak blessings over the desires of my heart. The Bible says He will provide for those, too. So believe in your promise, activate the power of your P, and begin to have faith in your God that He will not only take care of your needs, but also your desires. He will withhold no good thing from you, because you love Him!

Live righteous.

This is the second standard or prerequisite to truly experiencing God's favor. If you have faith, you should live your life as if you are living for Christ. Be righteous in your ways and remember that you represent Christ. James 2:18 (NLT) reads, "Now someone may argue, "Some people have faith; others have good deeds." But I say, "How can you show me your faith if you don't have good deeds? I will show you my faith by my good deeds." Show your faith by your good deeds. Your good deeds include praying and worshiping God, giving to His kingdom, helping others, and staying clear of immoral living. A guide to righteous living is the life of Jesus. He was there for the poor and those who were discounted. He was fair. He didn't judge or torment people for their wrongs. Once we become injected with the Holy Spirit and begin to seek God's guidance daily, righteous living becomes our way of life. It becomes natural to us, and we get better at it as we become more consistent in our journey.

Experience favor.

If you have faith and live righteously, you will experience God's favor. This is the most simple equation, yet many aren't able to leave their own wants behind to live a favored life. Meditate on the verses below for a moment:

For the Lord God is a sun and shield; the Lord bestows favor and honor. No good thing does he withhold from those who walk uprightly.

Psalm 84:11

And the Lord will guide you continually and satisfy your desire in scorched places and make your bones strong; and you shall be like a watered garden, like a spring of water, whose waters do not fail.

Isaiah 58:11

In him we have obtained an inheritance, having been predestined according to the purpose of him who works all things according to the counsel of his will.

Ephesians 1:11

For his anger is but for a moment, and his favor is for a lifetime. Weeping may tarry for the night, but joy comes with the morning.

Psalm 30:5

Blessed are the pure in heart, for they shall see God.
Matthew 5:8

Your purity through your body, your mind, and your spirit will allow your heart to be pure as well, so that you may become an empty vessel for God to fill with His desires, His love, His care, and His favor. Your journey is predestined and you have an inheritance to capture. As you move through your journey toward your promise, with God as your captain, you will not fail. There will be new gifts uncovered and opportunities that you will discover. Your wants and your needs will be taken care of—abundantly.

Repeat.

Once you get wrapped up in the faith cycle of trusting and believing God for things, living life according to His word, and receiving favor in your journey, you will become addicted to the lifestyle. You will grow more and more in your faith and trust God enough to KNOW that He will provide favor for your journey. This is how strong I want your faith to be. Now, my husband and I are so strong in our faith that we have begun to trust God to enlarge our territory. Our faith is so big and any doubt that once was has been removed. Trust and know God enough to realize that you don't have to play small anymore. You don't have to be shy or timid about your purpose in God's kingdom. You don't have to hide from your past or even the present dangers that will rise up against you. God's got you, and He has and will provide favor for your journey.

Below I want you to think deeply about this chapter, about the miracles and blessings God has provided you —because if He did it before, He can and will do it again. List the specific areas in your life that you are trusting God for. What

122

favor do you need for your journey?

I am trusting God to provide favor in my journey over:

1. My health

_____

_____

_____

2. My spirit

_____

_____

3. My wealth

_____

_____

_____

4. My relationships

_____

_____

_____

5. My finances

_____

_____

_____

6. My purpose

_____

_____

_____

My Eleventh Power Source - God's Favor

God provides favor for those who live for Him and those who care about His people. For every obstacle I face, God has already given me dominion.

Purity Prayer

Dear Lord,

You are holy and righteous in all of your ways. I pray that my thoughts become your thoughts, my desires become your desires, and my faith grows strong enough to activate your favor. Lord send me where you need me to go, to who I'm assigned and I will press forward to complete the journey, knowing that you have already predestined your favor to follow me wherever I go. In your holy name, Amen.

Purity Promise

Today, I promise to lose fear and doubt and instead live and walk in faith, live righteously and in my God-given assignment, so that I can abide in His love, grace, and favor, forever.

Chapter 12
Dream Wedding

An excellent wife who can find? She is far more precious than jewels.
Proverbs 31:10

My wedding day was a dream come true. It was hard for me to sleep the night before, because I was nervous, excited, and anxious—you name it. I knew that the next day would be a fantasy come true. I would stand before my king, God, my family, and the entire congregation and marry my best friend. The morning of my wedding, I read a book that my friends put together. It was one of the sweetest gifts I've ever received!

I was so calm and ready, yet excited and at peace. I truly wanted to enjoy my wedding day, so each chance I got I would pause and take it all in. At 7 a.m., we started all of the prep work, including hair, makeup, taking pictures, getting dressed. Tim and I were texting each other until 11 a.m.! It was the sweetest thing. We were so happy, confident, and ready to start our lives together. The wedding began at high noon on 10.10.15 at First Baptist Church of Glenarden in Prince George's County, Maryland.

My bridesmaids consisted of my closest friends and family and my sister Brittney, who was my matron of honor.

They were all so beautiful. It was amazing to share my last moments as Brelyn Freeman with women who watched me grow and poured into my life so much. Soon the time came, to walk down the aisle! Surprisingly, I didn't get nervous until the doors opened and I was standing there looking at everyone, over 2,500 people, who were all staring at me. Tim came up with the most beautiful music arrangement for me to walk down the aisle to— it was a mixture of "Ava Maria" and "Here Comes the Bride" (OMG, it was so beautiful). My dad was literally crying his eyes out. I was helping him down the aisle (lol). As I walked closer to the altar, Tim began to sing. I heard him singing the words, "I believe in you and me..." and I couldn't believe I was able to hold back tears. Although there were so many tears of joy around me, I wasn't crying yet! But then, my dream was elevated!

The one and only CeCe Winans started singing "For Always." How could I not cry in that moment? I felt the tears filling and my eyes and I couldn't hold them back. I LOVE CeCe Winans, and since I was a young girl, I've always dreamed of her singing at my wedding. It all hit me at once that this was really real! I was so grateful to be in that moment. I knew, right then, that I was a queen. Here I was walking the final few steps to meet my king, as my father held me close, my friends and family snapped pictures, and one of my favorite artists of all time ushered me into the rest of my life. I was so humbled and honored that God heard my prayers. This was what I'd always wanted.

My mind was racing with excitement, but I was focused on was being grateful in that moment and soaking it all in. I truly didn't want to miss a thing. My wedding day was honestly a dream come true, one that girls imagine and pray for. I knew that my prayers had been answered and, standing there taking my vows, my life was being rewarded by God and celebrated by my family. I knew that my values and purpose were not in vein. It was finally real. God sent me my king and He answered my prayers. He was demonstrating the rewards of a righteous lifestyle, a purity lifestyle, before the world. There were between 2,500 and 2,800 guests at my wedding, and the services were streamed online as well. It was really a holy production.

The day of my wedding, Tim gave me an engraved ring box and tray as a wedding gift. He knows me so well. I'm the sentimental type and I loved his gift so much. It's something I will treasure for the rest of my life and pass it on to our children and grandchildren.

Despite how incredible our wedding ceremony was, it was my reception that made the news. The huge surprise that I had for my father on the day he gave me away went viral. I presented a purity certificate, signed by both my doctor and myself—confirming for my father that I had saved myself until my wedding day. The doctor had confirmed that my hymen was in tact. Although my sister did the same thing years before, it wasn't something that was required, and so it wasn't expected! I wanted to make the same statement I'd been making since I was thirteen years old. I presented the purity certificate to my dad to confirm for him and the world that I believed and practiced what I had been talking about for years.

Prior to my wedding day, I talked the talk, but on that day, I proved that I had in fact walked the walk. I've always been a person that does the most, goes overboard, and shows out. So everything about that presentation and statement matched my personality to a T. Although some people at the reception were shocked, I wasn't concerned about what people thought about it. I knew that what I was doing was a GOD thing, and no one could talk me out of it.

My story has since been featured all over this nation from Good Morning America, The Doctors, Nightline, syndicated radio, and dozens of Christian, gossip, and lifestyle websites. My simple decision to honor God publicly proved an important point about how He works, and it demonstrates what God is trying to do for you. He's trying to show off your life as a trophy to the world that says, "This is what a child of God looks like!"

If you have a dream, believe it. If you're doing it big for God, spread the news. If you know your promise, keep that in sight. Don't be afraid to proclaim your faith, believe your big dreams, and parade your answered prayers around for all to see. Besides, you've exercised and activated the power of your P, and God wants nothing more than for you to honor Him by proclaiming your faith to the world. God delivers on our answered prayers and makes our dreams come true so that we can be a witness for Him.

Expect Controversy

When you are doing something unthinkable and going against the grain, don't be surprised at the backlash you will receive. When your dreams come true and you begin to walk in your full purpose with God, some people will support you, but others will try to break you, test you, and make you feel as though what you're doing isn't a big deal. Here's the thing though—it is. You are a big deal. God is a big deal. Your answered prayers and your righteous living is a big deal, and you deserve all of the favor that will follow after you've reached a new level of success as a result of honoring God. After my dream wedding, Tim and I were on our honeymoon and all at once, almost as if it were planned and timed, our phones began to beep and buzz and ring simultaneously.

The picture of my dad and I with my purity certificate

went viral. People were inboxing me on Instagram, retweeting the gossip sites, posting comments, and texting me. Although I didn't expect people to find any fault in what I did and the big statement that I made at my wedding, they did. In my eyes, I was honoring God with my decision. I was proving the point that it *is possible* to date and live in purity, to honor God, to save yourself until marriage. It's also possible for a man to save himself for his wife. I felt the message Tim and I were sending is one that's needed and was missing in today's sexually motivated society. No one has a problem with media that parades promiscuity and celebrates sexual openness. I didn't get why so many people were attacking our decision.

Regardless of my feelings, the controversy had hit. People found fault in me. They thought I was condemning women. Some people posted comments about how what I did was a private matter, and it shouldn't have been celebrated publicly. Others thought I was giving false hope about virginity and purity. Some people attacked my age or attributed my virginity to growing up as a preacher's kid. The naysayers found every reason to be hypocritical, instead of focusing on the one reason why no criticism was needed: my purity presentation adhered to the Word of God.

I know that my decision made others feel some type of way about the choices they had made or the life they were living, and that's okay. It's okay to cause controversy, when you are honoring God. God proved through us, that *yes it's possible*, and voila—here's proof! Remember that story I told you in Chapter 2 about Queen Esther? She was a regular girl, who was elevated to queen, as a virgin. God did it back then, and here He goes doing it again. It is still possible to live pure and God will reward that decision.

After we returned from our honeymoon, Tim and I received requests from all over the country to come on various media outlets to speak about purity. Many of the journalists wanted to find fault in our dream wedding and our decision to parade our purity to the world and honor God through our bold statement, "Save yourself, don't protect yourself." Many of the journalists picked and prodded and wanted us to say something—anything—that was negative. What they found instead was a perfectly happy couple, who honored God in mind, body, and soul. I think some of them may have felt like we were a little "too perfect."

We don't claim to be perfect, but we are a perfect example of what God will do. The more and more I was attacked, the more journalists wanted interviews, and they kept us trending. At one point, Tim and I had been included in Christian radio personality Willie Moore Jr.'s top stories for three days in a row, on his nationally-syndicated Christian radio show. The more criticism and controversy that came, the more requests I received to speak, the more people began to Google Tim's song and increase the plays on his videos, the more people visited our website and purchased purity gear. In short, the more people talked, the more glory God received. It also drew me closer to God and made me rest and abide in Him more.

This time also brought my family closer together, and allowed Tim and me to realize the real reason for our ministry. Our ministry gave people hope. Our life proved that the devil is a liar. God's Word is still prevalent today, and His promises are real. Even through the controversy, we began to receive some of the most beautiful declarations of faith. The power of the P was in full effect. Girls and women started contacting me telling me that they too were virgins, and thanking me for speaking out about this topic. Others were requesting resources and support for how to live a life of purity even after they had sex, and others wanted to continue the pu rity movement. This is why I felt writing this book was necessary. I realized that God's plan was bigger than Tim and me. He wanted me to help those who are also on this path, or those who want to be, to create a plan of action.

I had to provide hope from my own personal testimony. So once my family realized what God was doing, the Holy Spirit spoke to us and instructed us to make it eternal, official, and provide the tool. This is why *No Ring, No Ting* was important. I yearned to tell the story — the *It's more than a virgin* story. I needed to tell the story and provide the blueprint for mothers, daughters, wives, girlfriends and single women who have a deep desire to honor God and experience the favored, blessed, and promised life. My dream wedding and my answered prayers are testaments for you, that your prayers can and will also be answered if you trust and believe in God and honor Him with all of your heart and soul.

If you believe that God has included your life to include a wonderful, purpose-filled marriage, I urge you to hold on to that promise, while empowering yourself and improving your relationship with God.

Clean the clutter from your life to indicate that you have room for someone else. Start to become what you seek in a mate. If you want someone who is emotionally healthy—become emotionally healthy. If you want someone who loves God more than anything on earth, than you begin to love God more than anything on earth. If you want someone who gives, than you become a giver. Whatever you want, become. You will attract what you're ready for and who you are. God will elevate you in every step of your journey, and when you're ready, He'll send you the person who can love and adore you—the person who is ready for you and the amazing, virtuous woman of God that you've become. Believe in your dreams. Don't give up hope, and until your dream man comes, make your relationship with God the greatest love story ever told.

The List
Below write your list of an ideal mate, and pray for God to guide you and implant His desires and will into your heart. Then, create a list of what would make you an ideal wife to your ideal husband.

_____

_____

_____

_____

_____

_____

To be an ideal wife, I will be/become:

_____

_____

_____

_____

_____

_____

My Twelfth Power Source - The Greatest Love Story - with God

My relationship with God is the greatest love story ever written. I will seek Him more and more, and trust Him to provide me with the desires of my heart. When the time is right, I know He will send the right person that will love me unconditionally and who will work in conjunction with me to honor God.

Purity Prayer

Dear Lord,

Thank you for loving me. Your Word instructs me to delight myself in you, and you will give me the desires of my heart. I'm trusting your Word and standing on your promises. You know my desires concerning love, relationships, and marriage, and I have faith that you will prepare me as I delight in you as you simultaneously prepare me for a life in marriage, if that is in your will. In your holy name I pray, Amen.

Purity Promise

I promise myself to make my requests known to the Lord, and cultivate the loving relationship that I have with Him, daily.

Chapter 13
Exceedingly and Abundantly

Now to Him who is able to do exceedingly abundantly above all that we ask or think, according to the power that works in us, to Him be glory in the church by Christ Jesus to all generations, forever and ever. Amen.
Ephesians 3:20-21

Are you ready to enter your place of abundance? If so, I invite you to follow me down a road of **faith** toward your promised land.

Hebrews 11:1 tells us that faith is confidence in what we hope for and assurance about what we do not see. People with great faith have developed it through a constant cycle of exercising the faith process as it pertains to various situations in their lives. Others develop faith simply because they have the ability to trust God. And then there are some people who realize their faith after going through a seemingly impossible situation or life crisis in which all hope seems lost and then God in all of his greatness saves the day and delivers them from the hands of the enemy. It becomes easier to trust that God will provide for our needs and our hearts' desires after we've experienced the benefits of our faith over and over again. In church, there's a common saying, "If He did it be fore, He can do it again." This is what I want you to remember. For a moment, I want you to think about the impossibilities that you've accomplished.

Perhaps you are:
The first person in your family to graduate from college
The first in your circle to own a business
The girl who made it out of the dire circumstances of your youth or neighborhood
A survivor—of anything

Perhaps God has:
Made a way for you out of no way
Given you strength to do things that you never imagined
Cured you or your loved one from some terrible illness
Saved you in the midst of a huge accident
Provided a meal for your table when your paycheck ran out
Restored your spirit and healed you after a terrible breakup
Spared you from consequences you deserved, after you did something you had no business doing
Blessed you with a person who opened your eyes to new possibilities

No matter what your life looks like or how old you are, there has been *significant* evidence of God working things out for your good—at every stage in your life, every single day. Remember when I said that we have to be sure to attribute our blessings to God, and not luck or another human being? When you want to increase your faith, this practice will be key. If you're having a hard time figuring out how God has blessed you constantly and in every situation, you may want to get a journal to begin documenting these blessings and how your faith has increased as a result. Start to write down what you pray for, how God answers your prayers, the ways God delivers for you, and how your trust in Him grows in various areas of your life.

To those with little faith, the thought of putting trust in God over *everything* feels similar to jumping out of a plane with no parachute, or walking a tight rope with no safety net below. It's point blank SCARY. But to those who have strong faith, God is our parachute and safety net. We know that we can step out on faith when the spirit tells us to, and that God will provide. The goal is for you to move from having little faith to strong faith.

God is well-aware how it can sometimes be difficult for us to exercise our faith, it is only mysterious to those who don't understand faith. Besides, we're humans—operating on earth, consumed by fleshly desires. And faith is a spiritual phenomenon. Trust me when I tell you that He understands how difficult it is for someone to have faith who doesn't have the spirit inside of them. Because it's not an easy concept and very extraordinary to do for the average person, God does a few things to help us exercise our faith. The first tool He gives us is an advocate: the Holy Spirit.

He instructs us to abide in His Word and tells us that if we do so, He'll give us perfect peace. He tells us that if we trust him, we can ask for anything in His son's name, and it shall be given—we can even ask Jesus to increase our faith as the disciples did in Luke 17:5. This is our first resource, a holy helper. Secondly, God rewards us for our faith. Because faith is very spiritual and not at all earthly, God rewards us when we exercise our faith and **choose** to operate in spirit. Why? Because when we do, we give Him room to work and show off how amazing He is. We make the principles of the Bible real today when we walk in faith and He's able to show and prove. This public display of faith, God's rewards, and our testimonies help win more disciples to the kingdom of God. In *My Answered Prayers* and *Favor in Your Journey* chapters, I shared with you the ways that God rewarded my faith and the choice I made to believe in His promises for me. I exalted the promise, and God clearly gave me favor. He rewarded Tim and me with the desires of our hearts (a happy, God-centered marriage and life fulfillment) because we trusted Him to do so.

We had faith in His Word and believed His promises. We activated the power of the P through our faith and God still rewards us because we made a conscious decision. God did the same thing for my sister, Brittney, and her husband, Kevin Borders. They too had faith in the promises of God, dedicated their lives and bodies to Him, and were rewarded exceedingly and abundantly more than what they could've imagined. Part of their big reward from God is the blessing of their twin daughters, my beautiful nieces.

One of the first examples of a faith journey is the story of Abraham that begins in the book of Genesis, which reads, *Now the LORD had said to Abram: "Get out of your country, from your family and from your father's house, to a land that I will show you. I will make you a great nation; I will bless you and make your name great; and you shall be a blessing. I will bless those who bless you, and I will curse him who curses you; and in you all the families of the earth shall be blessed."* - Genesis 12

God chose Abraham to be the first leader of our faith. But Abraham had to demonstrate his faith in order to reach his place of promise. The Jewish nation would arise through Abraham's descendants, and through this family line, the people would receive the covenant of the Lord. God promised that he would bless Abraham and his barren wife with a son who would have countless descendants, one of which—

138

Jesus— who would be the savior for the whole world. This promise seemed a bit far-fetched for Abraham and his wife, Sarah, because they were really old. They were probably thinking, how could she possibly give birth to a child? But Abraham still believed in God's promises.

Have you ever been faced with a promise or word from God that you wanted to believe Him for, but it just seemed impossible, based on your current circumstances? This is a sign that you should in fact believe. God loves to work wonders under desperate circumstances, 2 Corinthians 12:9 tells us that God's power is made perfect in our weakness. For many women who want to be married and have children, this promise *feels* more unrealistic and unlikely for them with each year and failed relationship.

After some time, instead of trusting God's Word and having faith in that promise, many people give up—or worse—decide to take matters into their own hands by choosing the wrong relationships, giving into pressure versus exalting their promise, and settling for second best or second place in someone's life. This was the case for Sarah. After years of waiting for God's promise of a child, Sarah (then Sarai) took matters into her own hands. She became so impatient that she asked Abraham to do the unthinkable—to have sex with her maidservant, Hagar, to get her pregnant. Abraham went along with his wife's wishes and slept with Hagar, who became pregnant and delivered a son named Ishmael. What Abraham and Sarah did is not unlike what many women do today.

We take matters into our own hands. We get side-tracked from the promise, because of the process of waiting and the time that passes. We lose faith in what God has promised us and we create situations that God has not ordained— then, just like Abraham and Sarah we have to deal with the consequences of operating outside of God's will. Maybe this isn't you. Maybe you're perfect in relationships, and always have been. But for a moment, I want you to think about all the women you know who have tons of potential—they have a promise from God attached to their lives. But instead of waiting on Him to work all things out, and give them that exceedingly abundant blessing of a dream husband and a fulfilled life, they settle for the knuckle-head.

They settle for being cheated on. They tolerate being played or mistreated, used, or abused. They soon find themselves in a cycle of heartache, worry, and regret (because of their wrong choices) and they need a deliverance. This is what Sarah did. After Hagar gave birth to Ishmael, Sarah became very jealous and began to treat her very badly. She even blamed Abraham for sleeping with Hagar! Before you judge Sarah or criticize her behavior, just think about how impatient you've been in the past, while waiting on God's promises. Think about the times when you took matters into your own hands. How did that work out for you? What did God do to show you that He was not pleased?

God was not pleased with Abraham and Sarah. They indeed suffered because of Sarah's impatience. Ishmael turned against Isaac, Abraham's son of promise, who was born thirteen years after Ishmael. Abraham was one hundred years old and Sarah was ninety when Isaac was born. God's promises still came to past, even though Abraham and Sarah made a huge mistake, and their path was not straight. Because they went astray, their road was tougher than it had to be. When I think about Abraham and Sarah, it reminds me so much of Christians today.

It becomes difficult for many of us to stay consistent and faithful while we're on the path to our promise. We get distracted by the process and the time. We often stray off path, and God becomes displeased. We make our journeys so much tougher than necessary.

I know that the problem here is a faith problem. This was the case with Sarah, and it's the case with many women today. Many lose faith as time passes, and we take matters in our own hands. Although God was upset with Abraham and Sarah, His grace surpassed their wrong, and as He said He would, He gave them a son of promise, Isaac. Throughout his life, Abraham constantly demonstrated his faith to God, even being willing to do the unthinkable—to sacrifice Isaac as an offering to the Lord. He went up to the mountain to offer Isaac as a burnt offering, as the Lord instructed, but just before he did, the Lord told him not to kill Isaac and gave him a ram for the sacrifice. Here we see Abraham's faith (Hebrews 11:17-19) and how God rewarded him for that faith. The Bible calls Abraham a friend of God:

'But you, Israel, are My servant, Jacob whom I have chosen, the descendants of Abraham My friend," Isaiah 41:8.

I'm not sure about you, but when God speaks about me, I want Him to consider me a faithful friend, just as he did Abraham. I desire to be a friend of God's. We have faith in our friends. We are loyal to our friends. We trust our friends. Do you trust God? Can He trust you, as He would a friend?

Obedience
To do what is right and just is more acceptable to the LORD than sacrifice.
Proverbs 21:3

Times that test our patience and require our obedience to God are often attached to a greater promise or reward that will not only benefit the person who is being tested, but others who are attached to that person as well. Our obedience to God is rewarded with a promise and payoff that surpasses any and every thing that we've lost. After we've remained faithful and obedient, God provides for us, exceedingly and abundantly—far greater than what we could have imagined. I think about Noah, for instance, who was given a great challenge by God—to save mankind. Thanks to Noah's obedience, every kind of land animal found refuge on the ark, and escaped the global flood. Noah's family was also saved, which meant the human species could live on and multiply.

This meant that Jesus Christ—the world's savior, would eventually be born as a descendant of Adam and Abraham through Noah. A great deal of heavenly pressure was put on Noah, and although he was afraid, he pushed past those feelings with faith and obedience that God had a plan for him. Another example that comes to mind is Job, who God tested and stripped of everything, yet even under pressure, Job didn't turn from God. Job had received so much bad advice from his friends—but he exalted his promise (and faith in the Lord) over the pressure from Satan and even his own wife, who suggested to Job, "curse God and die." But do you think Job budged? Not at all. As a result, God revealed the reasons for Job's suffering to him, and He blessed him with twice as much than he had before his suffering began. Job's story is an example for us all that God is with us even during adversity—and He never leaves us, no matter how dim our situations look. Most importantly, Job's story is an example of God's restoration power.

Okay, so here's a moment when I want you to reflect, or better yet, analyze your own thoughts and life. What seems impossible? What do you need God to restore in your life? What seems hopeless? Do you believe that God will restore that as well? Job's life is an example that He will do exactly what He said He would do—exceedingly and abundantly above anything you can imagine.

Next let's look at the life of our Lord and savior Jesus Christ himself. He stayed obedient to God throughout His entire life—never sinning, not even once. He knew His fate, and that He'd face a horrible death. He trusted His father and knew that He had to suffer and die in order to save the world from sin.

Imagine if Noah, Abraham, and Jesus had said, "Nah God, I'm good. I can't even go out like this. I'd rather just keep doing me." What if Jesus had chosen His own path, rather than facing His crucifixion? What if Jesus decided the temptation was too much too resist and what if He found an attractive Jewish girl, and decided to start dating her? I'm being serious—what if for one second Jesus went off path, off focus, and off of His promise? He would've altered the course of our existence. What if He decided to create His own life— get married, have kids, skip fasting, and let every man and woman fend for themselves—versus forging forth on the path that God designed for Him to save the world? Jesus' decision to remain consistent, exalt His promise over the pressure, and have faith in God, is the reason why you and I are alive and saved by grace.

Jesus understood the power of the P and He knew that obedience was better than sacrifice. Because He honored God and remained faithful to Him, God rewarded Jesus exceedingly and abundantly. Jesus' name is now honored throughout the earth—He sits at God's right hand and still acts as an intercessor, even here on earth. Can you imagine if Jesus didn't follow His purpose, and we had no protection against the enemy and no promise attached to our lives or earthly death?

What are the "what ifs" attached to your promise? *What will not happen if you don't do what God wants you to do?* It's that serious. Your promise is at stake, and you never know what mission on this earth God has for you. His word *does* say that all things work together for the good of those that love Him and are called according to His purpose.

Because you're reading this book, I know you're called. I know you have a purpose. Just like Noah, Abraham, and Jesus. What would have happened if Noah did not comply with God and did not produce offspring? I don't want to even think about this! Just as the obedience was attached to a greater promise for Jesus, Abraham, and Noah's life, there's a big promise attached to yours as well. Their promise, and yours too, can only be accomplished if you have faith in God and are obedient to God's call and purpose for you. Obedience is better than sacrifice.

Obeying when it's Hard

It can be hard to obey God when you are going against the grain. People often fear to obey because it often means you're signing up for public rejection. Remember, however, that when it's hard to obey, it's definitely worth it. God will reward your obedience. He will deliver those who are faithful to Him.

In the book of Daniel, we meet Shadrach, Meshach, and Abednego who were leaders in Babylon, under the rule of King Nebuchadnezzar. Back in those days, King Nebuchadnezzar required everyone to bow down to a golden statue, a false idol that he had created.

The king was so adamant about this that he put a law in place to punish all who refused to bow down. They were to be thrown into a fiery furnace for disobeying his law. This instilled fear into the people of Babylon. Daniel 3 notes that the princes, the governors, the captains, the judges, the treasurers, the counsellors, the sheriffs, and all the rulers of the provinces gathered to worship the golden statue.

But Shadrach, Meshach, and Abednego refused to bow

down to the statue. Even though they knew that they might die, these three holy leaders still chose to obey God rather than the king. Daniel 3:13 documents the king's response, "Then Nebuchadnezzar flew into a rage and ordered that Shadrach, Meshach, and Abednego be brought before him. When they were brought in, Nebuchadnezzar said to them, "Is it true, Shadrach, Meshach, and Abednego, that you refuse to serve my gods or to worship the gold statue I have set up? I will give you one more chance to bow down and worship the statue I have made when you hear the sound of the musical instruments. But if you refuse, you will be thrown immediately into the blazing furnace. And then what god will be able to rescue you from my power?" (NLT).

What happened next in Daniel 3:17-18 is one of the most profound and fearless acts of faith and obedience that I can ever imagine. Shadrach, Meshach and Abednego responded, "If we are thrown into the blazing furnace, the God whom we serve is able to save us. He will rescue us from your power, Your Majesty. But even if he doesn't, we want to make it clear to you, Your Majesty, that we will never serve your gods or worship the gold statue you have set up." This right here makes me want to praise God. Can you conceive facing death and standing for your beliefs, and betting your future on God, so confidently? They didn't budge and although they may have felt fear, they acted fearlessly.

They knew it was now or never, and they called on God to deliver on His promises. The king had the three men tied and thrown into the fire. Next thing he knew, he looked up and they were walking around in the furnace with a fourth man whom he said looked like a God. After that, Shadrach, Meshach, and Abednego were taken out of the fire, and the Bible says that not even a hair on their heads appeared to be affected by the flames. This was enough for the king. He or dered all the people to worship the God of Shadrach, Meshach and Abednego. They were also promoted in their positions at work. They trusted and believed and declared that God would in fact deliver them, and he did.

This story is an example that God will deliver for those who are obedient to His Word—even when it's hard. God still does this today, in our society. I urge you to take a stance for God. Maintain your position and do not waver, because the payoff for your faith and obedience is favor and elevation!

Partway Obedience

Are you one of those people who picks and chooses which parts of the Bible you'll apply to your life? If so, you're like the majority of society that believes they can be selective with God's instructions and direction. The world glorifies sin and makes it very easy to accept certain parts of the Bible and disregard others, based on our own personal feelings or wants. While God's instructions for us may not always be easy, and they aren't always want *we want,* they are what He wants for us. God is our father, and He knows what's best for us. And many Christians who feel that they are doing "good" deeds, fail to be obedient and therefore delay their promise or alter their futures altogether. Despite how much He loves us, He reserves the right to chastise us for not following His instructions, completely.

Consider the Prophet Moses, for example, whose phenomenal story we read in the book of Exodus. He was a great leader who God called to lead the Israelites out of Egypt after being in bondage for 430 years. Moses was a good leader and most of the time he did good deeds, exactly what God asked him to do. God empowered Moses to speak on His behalf, he led God's people, and performed miracles on behalf of God, including parting the Red Sea, so that the Israelites could make it to the promised land. God even gave Moses the Ten Commandments, which is the basic blueprint for Godly living, even today.

God had promised Moses that he and his brother, Aaron, would lead the Israelites into the promised land—and they did. However, because Moses made a decision to only obey God partly, Moses never had a chance to enter the land promised to the Israelites. How do you think he must've felt after dedicating forty years to being a shepherd to the Israelites based off of a promise—only not to reach that promise? This is what's happening today, over and over, in the lives of Christians. Here's the defining moment that altered the course of Moses' promise.

When Moses, Aaron, and the Israelites arrived at the Desert of Zin, the people started to complain about the lack of food and water to drink. Moses and Aaron prayed and asked God what to do. God promised Moses that if he gathered the people together and spoke to the rock, he would make water pour from the rock for the people to drink. Moses proceeded to obey God. He gathered his people together, but he did not speak to the rock. Instead he hit it twice with his staff. While God was unhappy with Moses' partway obedience, he still allowed the water to flow.

But Moses and Aaron paid the price for that decision. They never made it to the land they had been looking forward to seeing for years... Sad right? That's exactly what I thought when I first read and heard about Moses as a young girl. It taught me an important lesson—that we never know which one of our disobedient decisions will cost us our promise. This is so profound to me, because I see it play out over and over in the church and by observing society. We just don't know what God's plans are, and we don't know how He's planned to bless us. We never know what we're sacrificing when we choose to do what we want to do. Are you a bad person if you disobey God's commands? Probably not— Moses wasn't a bad man. He was a servant leader, a prophet, blessed and chosen by God to accomplish an amazing purpose for God's kingdom. Still one small decision cost him his promise.

Earlier I mentioned a problem with grace. Too many people abuse God's grace and we know that He'll forgive us, and so we commit pre-meditated sins, and expect God to fix our messes and restore our spirits when we do. If we can simply have faith and trust God that His will is the best way for us, and be obedient instead, we'd save ourselves so much heartache and pain, and be consistent in our purpose path and promise journey.

Pearls

"Don't waste what is holy on people who are unholy. Don't throw your pearls to pigs! They will trample the pearls, then turn and attack you.
Matthew 7:6

I'm of the belief that each woman is a gift from God to the earth—not just for men or our spouses and families, but for the entire earth. We possess a great deal of tenacity, courage, strength, wisdom, care, and delicacy. We are resourceful, beautiful works of art. We know that God is holy. We know that we are made in His image. We know that we are made for a specific reason, to accomplish a specific purpose and we have a holy promise attached to our lives. Everything about us is in fact special and holy and worthy of the best that God has for us. When I think about women in this way, it makes me wonder what needs to happen to make all women view themselves that way. I also wonder why we'd ever waste all of our greatness on what God has not prepared, ordained, or equipped for us? The answers are clear:

We don't care about how we appear in God's image.

We are weak in our flesh.

We have little faith that God has in fact created someone for us who is designed and equip to handle our pearls.

After reading this book, my prayer is that you no longer have a problem with 1, 2, or 3. This time that we've spent together was designed to make you care—to get you to understand your value and strengthen your spirit so that you can fight your weak flesh and have more faith in God's promise for you.

If we've accomplished our goals together, and you're in fact prepared and equipped to honor God with your whole mind, body, and spirit, it's only a matter of consistency and obedience. Will you be consistent? Will you be obedient? Will you draw closer to God every day so that He considers you a friend and provides not only your needs, but the desires of your heart as well? Notice I didn't ask *can* you be consistent or *can* you be obedient. I know you can. God has made you that way. Now it's simply about activating the power of the P that is already inside of you.

Will you?

Abundantly

Now unto him that is able to do exceeding abundantly above all that we ask or think, according to the power that worketh in us...
Ephesians 3:20

God is able to do more than you can imagine, if you simply activate the power that is working inside of you—the power of the Holy Spirit, the power of the blood of Jesus, the power of your promise that exceeds all of your wants, needs, and expectations. Remember this, and never again force another thing. Never beg for anyone's attention. Never cry over who doesn't want you, who has rejected you, or who doesn't notice you. Remember that God is able to do way more than what you ask or think, so ask Him for what you want. Remember the power that works inside of you is strong enough with God. Notice Ephesians 3:20 doesn't say that the power that a boyfriend or a husband gives you.

The power is *already* inside of you. I know that as you cleanse your entire being to become as pure in the flesh as you do in your mind and spirit, that power will be activated so strongly that you'll begin to attract the people and things that deserve you. Purpose attracts purpose. I'm praying that you stay strong on your purpose path as you work magic and miracles with the power of your P. May God bless you and strengthen you in all that you do.

Love,

Brelyn

My Thirteenth Power Source - God's Exceeding Abundance

I am waiting on God and trusting Him to provide far more than what I can ever think or imagine.

Purity Prayer
Dear Lord,
I am prepared to live my life for you, and honor you in mind, body and spirit. I am trusting on your Word—Ephesians 3:20—which says that you will provide exceedingly and abundantly more than I can think or imagine. I'm trusting in your Word that says you will provide the desires of my heart. I am trusting you to strengthen me with wisdom, faith, and courage as I live in purity. I ask for your everlasting love and strength and I will live in obedience, according to the path that you've set for me. Thank you in Jesus' name, I pray, Amen.

Purity Promise
I promise to call on my friend, God, when I am in need of strength and faith on my journey. I promise to live in and on purpose and to exalt God's promise for me over any pressure I may face.

For all of God's promises have been fulfilled in Christ with a resounding "Yes!" And through Christ, our "Amen" (which means "Yes") ascends to God for his glory.
2 Corinthians 1:20 (NLT)

Chapter 14

Purity Campaign

In the same way, let your light shine before others, so that they may see your good works and give glory to your Father who is in heaven.
Matthew 5:16

In 2008, when President Obama became the first black president of the United States of America, he did so by inspiring hope, mobilizing first-time voters, black people, and millennials, and by using social media to reach voters, like no other candidate had ever done. He had a well-organized campaign that spoke to the masses and inspired people with the simple message, "Yes We Can!" and a slogan, "Change we can believe in."

A campaign is defined as organized action to create change. A good campaign will inspire and connect people, change behaviors, and create new energy around a topic. A great campaign will include a community of engaged members who each believe in a common ideal(s) and have a shared means to communicate or speak with one another.

A campaign will inspire its own tribe of followers who will advance the campaign's message and wear its philosophies like a badge honor. Seriously, think about how many people you know who immediately purchased Obama but

153

tons, calendars, mugs, t-shirts and bumper stickers following his election in 2008. Great campaigns will inspire people and give them hope in something bigger than self. So how does the campaign creator ensure that their campaign will be successful? I have no doubt that every successful campaign has a leader who is focused on the end goal and consistent in the journey. The end goal must stay in clear sight.

My goal for years has been to create a change in thinking amongst my peers, those who are coming up after me and parents who are raising youth in today's society. This book, the t-shirts, and my work within the church have reinforced the honest-to-God truth, that purity is the best lifestyle. Our slogan is simple: "Save yourself, Don't just protect yourself." While many people can criticize the delivery style or message, you cannot deny the truth when it's based in God's word. There have been other purity campaigns in our history. Notably in the early 90's, soon after the HIV/AIDS epidemic demanded the nation's attention, *True Love Waits*, a purity movement that targets students, was launched at Youth Ministry National Conference in 1993 in Nashville, Tennessee.

Less than a year later, over 100,000 students had signed commitment cards, vowing to live in purity. A year after the campaign started, *The Christian Post* reports that more than 210,000 cards from teenagers pledging abstinence were displayed in the National Mall in Washington, D.C. The founders of *True Love Waits* found that God had in fact elevated their message and campaign to the masses. While the purity movement has raised awareness of the risks of premarital sex and honors God, it has also received a lot of criticism, including from Christians, media. and even those who took pledges and vows of sexual purity—but did not stay committed. The fact remains that we live in a sinful world, and many aren't able to uphold to the standards associated with public pledges of purity.

Disney stars such as Miley Cyrus, Selena Gomez, Demi Lovato, and the Jonas Brothers once wore their virginity like a badge of honor, but some chose to later abandon their purity pledges and ditched purity rings, admitting to having sex before marriage. When we live of the world and are consumed by it, it is difficult to maintain a spiritual standard for living. This is why we must constantly abide in God's presence and allow Him to direct our paths no matter what situation we end up in, be it on the cover of magazines and starring in movies or teaching a class at the local high school. We must consistently invite God into our hearts—and pray—to keep our promises and stay on our promise-driven paths. When we constantly fill our spirits with the Word of God, no matter where we end up, we will have a Word that we can pull out to tackle any of life's circumstances and obstacles.

Yes We Can.

Society would have us believe that it's impossible to remain abstinent and pure. Our lifestyles have changed so much and society embraces anything—including lifestyles that are in direct conflict with the Word of God. Gay marriage is legal. Living together is practically a prerequisite to marriage for many women. The number of unmarried adults that are currently cohabitating has increased tremendously in the past four decades. A 2013 survey by the Centers for Disease Control found that 48 percent of unmarried women were cohabitating (compared to 34 percent in 1995); 20 percent of those women said they were pregnant within a year. Pornography is also on the rise, and many Christians admit to having sex before marriage. A 2008 study, entitled *Cyber Psychology and Behavior,* found that 93 percent of boys and 62 percent of girls are exposed to Internet porn before the age of eighteen. A study entitled, *Teen Sexting and Its Association with Sexual Behaviors,* found that 28 percent of the teens who participated had sent a sext.

Statistics make sexual purity seem like it's impossible—the odds seem to be against you. However, I'm of the "Yes We Can" mindset on this issue. If we take the attention off sex, and put it on changing mindsets—renewal of the mind—as God instructs, we can have more success, despite negative influences and daunting facts around sex. The topic of purity has often been considered a white, Evangelical thing, not a minority urban thing—not a fresh, fly, and black thing. In doing some research on the issue, and listening to people discuss their attitudes towards sex, I'm not surprised. See, many parents avoid the topic of sex altogether, but they expect the church and the Bible to guilt youth into remaining abstinent. Youth cannot be "scared straight" or scared into purity, rather. Instead, we have to make sex a conversation that parents feel comfortable with having.

The benefits of sexual purity must be taught—not only the fear of its consequences. By now, I'm sure you realize that purity isn't just about abstaining from sex. It's about raising our standards, renewing our mind, honoring God and positioning ourselves for the promises of God. No matter your age or place in the journey, you can become and remain pure. It is possible. And when you have the right tools inside of you (the Holy Spirit) God will make you more than a conqueror. Flesh does not have to overtake you. You don't have to become a negative statistic.

The goals of *this* Purity Campaign are to raise awareness to the sad fact that standards have been lowered in the body of Christ, due to the desensitization of society. We also want to influence people to value their bodies, increase their self-worth and self-esteem through the word of God. Society has conditioned us to believe that if you're not having sex prior to being married, something is wrong with you. I would like to get people to flip this thinking and ask the more relevant question, "Why not wait?" When one doesn't value and honor themselves, nobody else will. They will constantly look for personal value through relationships. Oftentimes these relationships are not long-lasting or substantive.

Sex simply complicates a situation that can be really simple. It puts your relationship in your emotions and outside of your brain. Once that Pandora's box is open, we are open to so many other things—mentally, physically, and spiritually. On the topic of sex, the media has it all wrong. Those who promote purity are made to feel like they're sex shaming (or slut shaming) as some outlets have labeled it. Or, in comparison, Disney pop stars are over sexualized and marketed as hot virgin sex symbols—besides who doesn't want what they can't have? For those who are truly honoring their walk with Christ and are totally confident in themselves, the chatter doesn't matter. Just as people wear their sexual promiscuity or "freedom" as a badge of honor, those who are abstaining from sex and other unGodly behavior should wear their purity as a badge of honor. Instead what's happened is that virgins and those who live in abstinence often keep quiet, as a defense mechanism.

I realized this when my story broke national. I had various messages from women who were virgins and were thanking me for taking a bold position on this issue. It's not "cool" to be a virgin—and so while many adults have saved themselves for marriage, they don't discuss it. Society tries to "virgin shame" us into silence. Just as conservatives wanted to silence Obama and his message of hope and change or label it as just naiveté, society does the same thing to us. But

I'm of the "Yes We Can!" mindset. I know that if we are made to feel like they aren't an anomaly and actually begin to speak out about their decision to honor God with their bodies, we can create a domino effect and normalize purity.

This Purity Campaign is about getting people to understand their worth by drawing closer to God and honoring their purity. Too many people give themselves away to others who do not deserve them. We share intimate parts of ourselves. We open up and become vulnerable. We, as a human race, fail to set the standards and our access at a high enough price. *No Ring, No Ting* is about treating your temple as a sacred place, and saving entryway into that temple for a sacred union, in order to carryout God's sacred purpose.

Purity is a philosophy that means more than virginity and it applies to more than singles. Even when we're married, we need to remain pure. When I think of purity, I think of wholeness and completeness—ready to be used. When you look up the word "purity" you will find what purity is. Purity means being free from contamination and pollutants, and free from evil and guilt and condemnation. So in fact, purity means that you are free from anything that can defile or make you unsuitable to be used for things that require cleanliness—Godly things or God's purpose for you.

When I say "wholeness" in relationship to purity, I mean wholeness in mind (or soul), spirit, and body. It starts with the mind and soul. If your thoughts become pure, a pure life is easier and attainable. If we remind ourselves of the statistics mentioned earlier about cohabitation, sexting, and pornography (and others that I didn't mention) you'll see why purity is about more than sex. Some singles mistakenly think that because they aren't being penetrated, they can still continue sexting, petting, humping, and grinding and still walk in purity.

Sin and uncleanliness is committed in the heart way before the act actually happens. Proverbs 23:7 (NKJV) says, "For as he thinks in his heart, so is he." Notice that this scripture does not say, you are what you do. Contrarily, we are what we think. You can do a lot of good for people, or better yet, you can serve God, work in the church, and serve others, but not have God in your heart. Your heart can still be impure—as is the case for many singles and married people, alike. If your heart and mind aren't pure, you will fall to sexual sins such as sex before marriage, and possibly lust or adultery, after marriage. *Christianity Today International*, Winter 2005 published the results of a survey with pastors, which cited the eight top sexual issues damaging their congregations.

They were:

57% pornography addiction

34% sexually active never-married adults

30% adultery of married adults

28% sexually active teenagers

16% sexual dissatisfaction

14% unwed pregnancy

13% sexually active previously married adults

9% sexual abuse

Married Christians aren't immune to impurity, because it's a matter of consistency, while consistently renewing our minds and allowing God to use us. Notice that there was only a 4 percent difference between sexually active never-married adults/singles (34 percent) and married adults who struggled with adultery (30 percent). Those who are married are not immune to the purity conversation. When you are impure as a single, you'll have a tougher time remaining pure within marriage.

As you can see, there are so many vulnerabilities di

rectly related to impurity—these can affect us no matter our religion, age, marital status, or virginity status. While I could've written an entire book to try and convince you to flee from lust and sinful acts, this book is about more. It's about getting you to change the way you think. Once you raise the level of your thoughts, you won't lower the level of your acts.

Change we can believe in

Let's talk about the campaign—a Purity Campaign to cause a shift in mindsets and lifestyles. A campaign that exalts Christ and demonstrates the power of our P through purpose-filled living. In 2015, award-winning entertainer Ciara and her new boyfriend Seattle Seahawks Russell Wilson announced their decision to abstain from sex. When celebrities take bold stances for their beliefs in the name of Jesus, it's sure to receive a little hate, but more importantly, those declarations get people to discuss and consider a different way of living.

While the "unattainable virgin" became a popular marketing strategy for various artists in the '90s and '00s, the only PR ploy here is to bring attention to God and how e says we should live. When people who are well-known, whether international celebrities like Ciara, Brittney Spears and The Jonas Brothers or local celebrities—neighborhood figures or campus role models—perhaps like you—take a bold stand for God it can create conversation that leads to change.

So let's band together to cause a change in our culture. By living a God-centered life and demonstrating the fruits of your mental-spiritual-and physical purity, we can influence change, one person at a time. You might not be Ciara, but you have some influence, at least over one person. If everyone reading this book, who stands for God and believes in His promises, would be willing to take one person under your wing to share the importance of valuing virginity or abstinence or for the married couples, to value the sanctity of marriage, we can win this fight. And don't get it twisted—we are in a fight.

We're in a fight for truth over lies. Righteousness compared to sin and light versus darkness. There are undoubtedly some who are blowing this message off as, "It's just sex. It's not that serious." My response? It takes just a small opening, and a snake can slither through, just as it only takes a little immorality to completely travel into a life of sin. Never forget that sin separates us from God, while purity brings us closer to Him. I'm not sure what else is more important than closeness to God. So if those of us who are up for the fight were to ban together, we can create a Purity Campaign that resonates with all ages, and puts Jesus on a pedestal. We can start a Purity Campaign with chapters across this world.

As we stand in our truth with the power of our P, we will allow criticism and doubt to motivate us to draw nearer to God—just as it did with me after my wedding. Hosts on the Dr. Drew Show said they didn't think it would become a trend for daughters to give their dads purity certificates at their weddings. I say to that, "Why not?" Not that it would be mandatory, but it would be a great 'big goal' for every young woman to strive for. **No matter where you are in your journey or walk with God, I invite you to join the campaign. Here are the first few steps:**

Visit meetthebowmans.com and download the purity certificate. Sign it and frame it and put it on your wall. If you're a virgin, sign a copy and have your dad or mom sign it with you.

If you're in a relationship, have a conversation about

abstinence with your significant other. Make it fun and perhaps you can start a running list of *Things to Do on a Date without Having Sex.*

Then, take one person under your wing—whether it's a little sister, friend, or mentee. Perhaps you and your friends can all take this pledge together.

Lastly, track your journey. Keep track of how your life has changed, how your relationship with God evolves and the answered prayers that you experience throughout your purity journey. Never forget that God rewards those who are obedient and honor Him, so you're definitely in for a few holy surprises.

The important thing to remember is to grow in Christ and stay connected to Him daily. When you are tempted by sex or things outside of God's will for you, pray. No matter what society tells us, and no matter how much impurity is promoted through media, I believe a Purity Campaign will create change we can believe in, and together, we can experience the ultimate promises of God, for ourselves, and our loved ones.

Your Campaign Trail: Write your answers to the questions below.

Are you ready to join the purity campaign? Why/why not?

Who will you invite on your journey with you?

What habits do you have to eliminate in order to be successful?

Listen, I know you can do it. Remember that God has already given you power and victory over temptation. There are so many negative statistics around sex. I'd love for us to cre ate new, positive statistics—stats that speak of fulfilled lives, saved souls, strong marriages, and signed purity certificates as a result of sexual abstinence. This is a campaign that you've been preparing for. If you've made it this far through the book, I have no doubt you have enough confidence, tools, and WMS (weapons of mass spirituality) stored inside of you to start the journey.

Join the campaign and save yourself for your future spouse. You are queen. Live like it.

My Fourteenth Power Source - I am Campaigning for God.

I am on a campaign for God to represent him and influence others. From this day forward, my life is a representation of a Christian who honors God, in mind, body, and spirit.

Purity Prayer

Dear Lord,
Please help me remain focused on my purity journey and honoring you. Please strengthen me and fill me with the Holy Spirit as I speak and influence others to live righteous. In Jesus' name, I thank you. Amen.

Purity Promise

I promise to become a witness for God and use my story of faith and strength as a testimony to God's glory.

How did *No Ring, No Ting* help you?

Follow @BreFree on Instagram and share your thoughts and updates about your journey with Brelyn. Visit meetthebowmans.com to get your purity gear, download your purity certificate or find additional resources about living for Christ.